Long-Legged
WADING BIRDS
of the
NORTH AMERICAN WETLANDS

Photographs by
LUCIAN NIEMEYER

Text by
MARK RIEGNER

Long-Legged WADING BIRDS *of the* NORTH AMERICAN WETLANDS

STACKPOLE
BOOKS

To my wonderful wife, Joan,
who loves the wetlands and finds peace in them.
LUCIAN NIEMEYER

To my parents,
who nurtured my love of nature.
MARK RIEGNER

Photographs copyright © 1993 by Lucian Niemeyer
Text copyright © 1993 by Mark Riegner

Published by
STACKPOLE BOOKS
Cameron and Kelker Streets
P.O. Box 1831
Harrisburg, PA 17105

All photos by Lucian Niemeyer,
with the exception of pages 38–39 by Joan Niemeyer,
page 92 by Linda Charamella, and page 152 by William Weber

Interior layout by Nai Y. Chang

Jacket Front: Great Blue Heron
Jacket Back: Roseate Spoonbill
Frontispiece: White Reddish Egret

Library of Congress Cataloging-in-Publication Data
Niemeyer, Lucian.
    Long-legged wading birds of the North American wetlands /
    photographs by Lucian Niemeyer; text by Mark Riegner.—1st ed.
        p. cm.
    Includes bibliographical references and index.
    ISBN 0–8117–1889–1
    1. Charadriiformes—North America. 2. Ciconiiformes—North
America. 3. Wetland ecology—North America. 4. Wetland conservation—North America. I. Riegner, Mark. II. Title.
    QL696. C4N54 1993
    598' .33—dc20   92–2854
                                                                 CIP

Printed in Hong Kong

First Edition

10 9 8 7 6 5 4 3 2 1

CONTENTS

Acknowledgments

Every species in nature has a role to play in its environment. In the forest, order is observed easily as animals and plants interact with each other and with air, water, and earth. The result is a symphony of life, with each part having a distinct and clearly definable role in the stage production. Each is dressed in precisely the correct garb and plays in a harmonious manner.

The wetland environment is the opposite, displaying a busy discordant carnival of life, enacting the individual spheres of each actor's realm, playing in the three-ring circus above, on, and below the water surface. There is a calliope of sound and color, with order seemingly absent. Yet, the more one takes the time to observe the pandemonium, the more one sees that each transaction is no less orderly or less important to nature than any other predictable natural phenomenon. It is only condensed to a small area with many interactions in a very close sphere of influence. A human being is bitten by a mosquito, which in turn is eaten by a frog, which ends up being devoured by a snake, which is then found in the stomach of a heron, which is eaten by an alligator, which eventually dies. Then the cycle repeats itself. Something is always going on, leaving the serious observer with a predicament of choosing which action to follow.

In many ways wetlands can be inhospitable to humans with their abundant insect life, humidity, stench of decaying matter, and oppressive heat. Yet, wetlands are the most important of nature's incubators, as the sun and wetness give sustenance of life in abundance and in concentrated form. Wetlands give the naturalist the easiest laboratory in which to observe and record the steps of the food chain—and the resulting life cycles—up close, with conclusions. The ecological quality of wetland environments represents humanity's success in preserving a balanced and healthy earth. For this reason we, as the one species able to determine a course of wetland health, must preserve wetlands in quality and quantity if we want to inhabit this earth as we have in the past. All nature is interdependent.

In bringing you this book, we are giving you one perspective of wetland conditions in North America: a study of the long-legged wading birds. We show and explain twenty species, five morphs, and several phases, each with its own distinctions. Hopefully this will create a thirst for more knowledge of wetland ecology and, above all, respect and care for the wetlands.

This book would not have been written without the encouragement of my wife, Joan, and my friend Leo Lamer. Many experts helped find the locations of different species: Jesse Grantham, Andy Tirpak, Rich Paul, and Sandy Sprunt of the Audubon Society. The National Park services of Pat Tolle and John Ogden were extremely helpful, as were the Platte River Trust's John Vanderwalker and Gary Lingle. Ted and Bobbi Appell of Rockport, Texas, with the *Skimmer* were especially helpful and the "teddi" coloration of the Reddish Egret is designated by me for Ted's help in recording it.

In addition, I want to thank Tanya Parsonage of the Delaware state park system and Roger Tory Peterson for his timely suggestions. There are three pictures not of my authorship: William Weber's lovely portrait of the Sandhill Crane on page 152; Linda Charamella's excellent picture of the white-phase immature Little Blue Heron on page 93; and Joan Niemeyer's wonderful picture of Atchafalaya Bayou on pages 38–39. I also appreciate Russell Peterson's foreword, especially as he has been such an outspoken proponent for the environment's health for so many years.

Mark Riegner's wonderful text and insights, combined with his sensitive consultation, have brought special significance to this work. Finally, I wish to thank all those flying and wading actors and their stage crews for their magnificent performances and the beautiful natural sets.

LUCIAN NIEMEYER

I thank Lucian Niemeyer for his numerous helpful suggestions, which improved the quality of the text. I am also grateful to the many friends who have accompanied me on natural history excursions and ramblings throughout the years. I am especially indebted to the late professor Robert E. Smolker, whose expertise, encouragement, and friendship guided me through my graduate research on wading birds. And finally, words are inadequate to convey the deep appreciation I feel toward the birds and wetlands that I have been fortunate to observe. May wild places, and the living things that are a part of them, survive into perpetuity!

MARK RIEGNER

FOREWORD

There is no better place to observe and enjoy the wonder, beauty, and variety of nature than in the world's wetlands. There is no better way to explore and appreciate the wetlands' rich biological treasures than by following the activities of the long-legged wading birds that grace these environments.

Lucian Niemeyer and Mark Riegner have done this work for you in their production of *Long-Legged Wading Birds of the North American Wetlands*. They have combined their considerable talents, love of nature, and many years of observation to create a strikingly beautiful and highly informative volume. The photography is outstanding, capturing all twenty of the North American species of these magnificent birds, displaying their various nuptial and feeding activities in their special habitats. The artists take the reader on a tour of the wetlands in key wildlife refuges in pictures and words, effectively describing the interdependence of the many species of life in these teeming sanctuaries, aided by the study of the long-legged wading birds.

This book will convince the skeptic that marshes and swamps are not useless wastelands. It will provide the expert with illuminating observations of the habits and characteristics of long-legged wading birds. And it will entice the novice to explore and enjoy neighboring wetlands with a new perspective.

Some of the world's most spectacular wetlands are in North America. What a rewarding experience it is to visit them. Such experiences, however, will not be available for future generations if we do not stop our assault on these important refuges of life. Ever more humans demanding ever more resources have been draining, filling, and poisoning these important incubators. More than 50 percent of the wetlands existing in the lower forty-eight states in colonial times have been destroyed. This tragedy is symbolic of the planet-wide assault by humans on all of the earth's life-support processes. It is urgent that we understand and teach, so as to reverse these life-threatening trends.

Each of us can make a difference. Each of us can help to save life in the wetlands. *Long-Legged Wading Birds* shows us why we must do so now.

Russell W. Peterson
President Emeritus - National Audubon Society
President Emeritus - International Council for Bird Preservation
Former Governor, Delaware

INTRODUCTION

At once familiar and mysterious, wetlands form an integral ecological network throughout North America. Their familiarity rests, in part, in their common inhabitants: Red-winged Blackbirds, fiddler crabs, clams, and water lilies. Yet these same well-known life forms open windows to the mysteries of the wetlands: what compass guides the annual migrations of the blackbird? What directs the claw-waving antics of the fiddler crab? How does the clam experience its world? What orchestrates the daily opening and closing of the water-lily blossom?

Since the early days of European settlement, North American wetlands have been misunderstood, maligned, and mistreated. More recently, however, knowledge and appreciation of the inner workings of these ecosystems have been growing and conservation efforts have been initiated. Nevertheless, wetlands continue to be destroyed, and they remain one of the most threatened ecosystems on the continent.

Wetlands, which include marshes, swamps, bogs, ponds, and streams, are defined by the U.S. Fish and Wildlife Service (1979) as, in part, "lands transitional between terrestrial and aquatic systems where the water table is usually at or near the surface or the land is covered by shallow water." In addition, Section 404 of the 1977 Clean Water Act Amendments defines wetlands as "those areas that are inundated or saturated by surface or ground water at a frequency and duration sufficient to support . . . a prevalence of vegetation typically adapted for life in saturated soil conditions."

As clear as these statements are, there is still a part of every wetland that evades definition, especially whenever a wetland touches a human life. How can one satisfactorily define the sunset glow over an estuary, the early vernal chorus of spring peepers in a pond, or the delicate dance of mayflies at a stream bank? The communication of these aesthetic experiences can only be partially accomplished through words. To help complete the circle, a pictorial approach is necessary. Accordingly, this is a book of words and pictures—a shared attempt to convey both an understanding and an appreciation of wetlands.

Wetlands are diverse in kind and complex in nature; thus, we have selected just one facet of wetland life to anchor our observations and to serve as our aesthetic focus—the long-legged wading birds. In our view, there are few wetland inhabitants that rival our selection in beauty, general interest, and conspicuousness. These birds, therefore, form the subject of this book, a subject we will explore within the context of the birds' wetland habitats. We want to show that wading birds and wetlands, organisms and environment, form an inextricable whole,

Dawn over Florida Bay as seen from Flamingo Point, Everglades National Park.

and that one cannot be fully understood or appreciated without the other.

The twenty wading-bird species featured in this work belong to the following families: Ardeidae (herons, egrets, and bitterns), Threskiornithidae (ibises and spoonbills), Ciconiidae (storks), Aramidae (Limpkin), and Gruidae (cranes). The characteristics that link together this somewhat diverse array include long legs, long necks, breeding in North America (north of Mexico), and a dependence on wetlands for survival. Although cranes are sometimes not considered waders in the strict sense, their reliance on wetlands for feeding and reproduction justifies their inclusion. Wetlands are also crucial to Cattle Egrets, although they do not necessarily venture into shallow water to feed. The Greater Flamingo qualifies as a long-legged wader, but in North America it appears only as a rare vagrant in southern Florida; therefore treatment here is unwarranted.

This book is a companion to field experience. We hope our readers will be stimulated to explore the waders of the wetlands and, after making field observations, return to these pages to broaden their understanding. Feeding behavior, reproduction, and migration are all described, but the former activity is given greater emphasis because foraging is the behavior most likely to be observed by a wetland visitor.

Only those wetlands that support a considerable abundance and diversity of long-legged waders are covered in this book. Thus, bogs, prairie potholes, and boreal wetlands, such as tundra, are not included, although they are certainly critical to waterfowl and shorebirds. For this same reason Canadian wetlands in general are not given strong consideration here even though Canada contains almost one-quarter of the world's wetlands.

1. The Wetlands, the Birds, and the Procurement of Food

PRECEDING PAGES:
Fresh water flows through the
Everglades into Florida Bay via the
eighty-kilometer-wide Shark
River.

T he predawn sky glitters in a tapestry of stars. Poised on this stellar stage, the gibbous April moon performs a spellbinding feat as it replicates itself into innumerable forms that dance on the water's surface. Barely visible, tightly clustered stalks of saltwater cordgrass, or *Spartina*, stand silhouetted against the shimmering surface. Here, in the silence of the morning, the presence of *Spartina* indicates the character of this place, a place where water and land merge into an indissoluble whole.

The air on this windless morning blankets the salt marsh with the pungent aroma of salt, muck, and the sweetness of decaying marsh grasses. In the dark galleries between the *Spartina* stalks, marsh crabs scuttle sideways. The maroon-colored crustaceans pause intermittently to bring particles of decomposing vegetation to their limblike mouths with robotic forelegs and claws.

Like the narrow mane of a great beast, salt marshes fringe much of temperate continental North America, especially along the Atlantic seaboard and the Gulf of Mexico. These wetlands are alternately inundated and drained, often twice a day, by advancing and retreating tides and have themselves advanced and retreated with rising and falling sea levels throughout the geologic history of the earth. Where the sea reaches into the mouth of a river, an estuary is born, such as in the Chesapeake Bay. The confluence of the sweet waters of the Mississippi River with the brine of the Gulf of Mexico in the Mississippi Delta creates the most extensive saltwater wetland system in the contiguous United States.

Powered by sunlight, the pulse of tides, and the importation of organic and inorganic matter, salt marshes are some of the most productive ecosystems on the planet. Much of their production is apparent in the luxuriant growth of *Spartina*, a singular group of grasses able to withstand saline water. Along the Atlantic coast two species of *Spartina* dominate salt-marsh landscapes: S. *alterniflora*, or cordgrass, and S. *patens*, salt-meadow hay. S. *alterniflora* can grow as tall as a man and is able to tolerate saltier water than its knee-high relative. Consequently, S. *alterniflora* establishes itself along the outermost margin of land and much of its stalk is submerged during daily high tides. In contrast, S. *patens* stands beyond the reach of all but the highest seasonal tides.

This zonation—an important feature of salt marshes—is further emphasized if additional marshland plants are considered. In a New

OPPOSITE:
A spring storm rolls into the *Spartina* marshlands at Anahuac National Wildlife Refuge near Houston, Texas.

13

Eastern Neck National
Wildlife Refuge, Chesapeake
Bay, Maryland.

England salt marsh, for example, plants are distributed from shore to high marsh as follows: cordgrass—spikegrass—glasswort—saltmeadow hay—black rush. This spatial sequence is influenced by the relative tolerance or intolerance of plants to salt water, as well as competition among species. Furthermore, the presence of the plants themselves modifies soil conditions and thereby affects the distribution pattern.

As fresh water drains seaward from streams and surface runoff and salt water flows landward with each ascending tide, row after row of *Spartina* stalks strain and capture suspended particles of vegetation and other matter. Subsequently, this material, and especially dead *Spartina* stems and leaves, enriches the ecosystem by fertilizing the plants and nourishing the marshland animals.

Spartina meadows and adjacent shallows may at first glance appear impoverished of animal life; however, close inspection on hands and knees reveals a diversity of life forms. Clams lie snugly ensconced in the mud, each leaving only a tiny, spurting breathing hole on the surface as evidence of the creature lurking below. Mussels and oysters silently huddle on creek banks, gently opening their shells to filter the nutrient-rich waters as the rising tide submerges them. Convoluted, pencil-thin tracks in the ooze indicate the presence of itinerant mud snails. In the upper intertidal zone, hordes of male fiddler crabs display outside their burrows, each crab jerkily, yet methodically, waving his one ridiculously overgrown claw to advertise his territorial possession and willingness to engage in matrimony.

Intertidal wetlands serve as year-round homes to hosts of marsh fish—mummichogs, silversides, killifish, minnows—and as temporary nurseries to others, such as mullet, striped bass, flounder, sea trout, and croaker. Many of these fish, as well as crabs, clams, and other invertebrates, fall prey to diamond-backed terrapins, raccoons, migratory shorebirds, and, of course, wading birds.

As dawn approaches, a soft glow appears on the eastern horizon and a veil of mist rises above the water's surface. The stars grow faint and forms begin to materialize on the marsh. In a distant tide pool, a Black-

Paurotis Pond is a freshwater wetland in Everglades National Park.

crowned Night-Heron stands in a hunched posture, patiently waiting for any movement in the shallow basin. The dark crown and back of this chunky heron contrast sharply with its ash-gray wings and creamy white head, neck, and underparts. It waits for about eight minutes, maintaining its crouched position, then takes six steps to the south and continues peering intently with its red eyes. Momentarily, it slowly extends its neck and stabs at the water. It quickly raises its head, and there, between its mandibles, squirms an eel twice the length of the night-heron's bill. As the heron vigorously shakes its prey, a piece of sea lettuce falls from its bill to return to the pool. After manipulating its serpentine meal for some time, the heron begins to swallow it head-first. Minutes later, just the eel's tail protrudes from the bird's bill and in a moment that, too, vanishes.

According to R.S. Palmer's classic *Handbook of North American Birds*, the Black-crown's preferred habitats are "so varied as to be diffi-cult to describe," and this bird is "adapted to nearly every conceivable habitat in which a wader might exist." Suitable environments range from fresh- to saltwater wetlands. Its diet is no less varied, including fish, frogs and other semiaquatic vertebrates, crabs, mussels, insects, and small mammals. In addition, Black-crowns take nestlings of other herons and of White Ibises and raid tern colonies. Concerning the lat-ter, night-heron disturbance occasionally has had devastating effects on tern reproduction by causing adults to abandon eggs and chicks. Black-crowns also have a reputation for pilfering fish hatcheries and other aquacultural establishments.

As its name implies, the Black-crowned Night-Heron is princi-pally a crepuscular and nocturnal hunter. Its Latin name, *Nycticorax*, means "Night Raven," a reference to its nocturnal habits and ravenlike call. Its large pupils enable it to see well in twilight or on moonlit nights. In tidal marshes and estuaries along the North Atlantic coast, this bird typically arrives on its feeding grounds at dusk and departs at dawn. When there are hungry nestlings to feed, however, the parents may forage even in daylight, especially under overcast skies.

Black-crowns hunt alone or in loose groups and establish feeding territories by defending an area within at least a two-meter radius. They usually either stand and wait for their prey to approach or stalk slowly after an unsuspecting quarry. Their more unusual feeding behav-iors include swimming, hovering, plunging, and bill vibrating (the rapid opening and closing of partially submerged mandibles), presum-ably to attract fish. Small creatures, such as minnows and insects, are snatched up and swallowed instantly. Larger prey, like the eel captured by this Black-crown in the marsh, may be manipulated for some time before they are positioned for swallowing. The larger the prey—and therefore the longer the handling time—the more likely it is for an individual heron to have its prize stolen by another Black-crown or, in daytime, by harassing gulls.

The Black-crowned Night-Heron (*Nycticorax nycticorax*) is a medium-sized (sixty- to seventy-centimeter), stocky, gray-and-white heron with a black crown, back, and bill, a red iris, and yellow legs and feet.

The salt marsh is now bathed in a golden light. The green-tinted water indicates a phytoplankton soup, a living broth of microscopic algae that drift with the ebbing and flowing tides. A raccoon hobbles along the water's edge, then exits behind a curtain of *Spartina*. A movement on a muddy embankment along a tidal channel reveals the presence of the Black-crown's close relative, the Yellow-crowned Night-Heron. In slow, deliberate steps, the Yellow-crown patrols the area for fiddler crabs, its favored prey. This slightly stocky heron is identified by its somber, bluish gray plumage, black head, and white cheek patches and crown, which are usually tinged with yellow. Its large reddish orange eyes are also distinctive. After taking several steps, the Yellow-crown remains motionless in an upright posture, its neck extended at a slight angle. Slowly, almost imperceptibly, it sways its head and neck in a steady hypnotic manner, gradually lowering for a strike. Then, in an instant, the bird jabs at a crab, clamping its stout mandibles around the crustacean. After swallowing the fiddler, the night-heron takes several paces within the crab colony to begin its vigil anew.

Known in some locales as crab-catcher, the Yellow-crowned Night-Heron is unique among herons in that it specializes in hunting and feeding on crustaceans such as crabs and crayfish, which can consti-

ABOVE LEFT:
Immature Black-crowned Night-Herons are sometimes mistaken for American Bitterns or immature Yellow-crowns.

ABOVE RIGHT:
Immature Yellow-crowned Night-Herons can be distinguished from Black-crowns by the formers' slightly heavier bill; the proximity of adults is also useful in field identification.

OPPOSITE:
The Yellow-crowned Night-Heron (*Nycticorax violaceus*) is a medium-sized (sixty- to seventy-centimeter), stocky, bluish gray heron with a yellowish white crown, black bill, orange iris, and yellow legs and feet. Ding Darling National Wildlife Refuge, Florida.

tute up to 95 percent of the Yellow-crown's diet. To manage such heavily armored prey, the night-heron has a moderately broad, deep bill, well suited to crunching up its victims. Although this heron is a specialist feeder on crustaceans, it will not hesitate to snap up anything manageable. Audubon lists the following items as part of the Yellow-crown's menu: snails, fish, small snakes, crabs, crays, lizards, leeches, small quadrupeds, as well as young birds that have fallen from their nests. I have observed Yellow-crowns eating small terrapins and have discovered the remains of beetles and the bones of mice and young cottontail rabbits at nest sites. As in other herons, Yellow-crowns regurgitate the undigested parts of their prey as pellets. Consequently, I have been able to collect hundreds of crab claws from beneath night-heron nests and subsequently identify the crab species in the Yellow-crown's diet.

Because of their nocturnal habits, Yellow-crowns are rightly considered night-herons. However, these wetland birds also may be active in full sunlight, especially in localities where tides determine prey availability. In nontidal areas night-herons typically search for food at dawn and dusk and on moonlit nights. Yellow-crowns usually hunt

In flight most herons, such as this Black-crowned Night-Heron, extend their legs and tuck in their necks.

alone, but sometimes small groups of independently hunting birds can be observed. Should one bird approach too close to another, violating its personal space of about two meters, the disturbed bird will perform a threat display. This performance consists of a slight retraction of the neck, raised crown and scapular plumes, and a partial opening of the bill, often accompanied by a hissing sound. Such a display usually suffices to send the intruder on its way.

The sun is now above the eastern horizon, quietly declaring its preeminence and significance to the salt-marsh ecosystem, for ultimately the sun is the source of all life that thrives here. *Spartina*, phytoplankton, and the algae that grow as a film on the muddy substrate require the sun's radiant energy to photosynthesize—that is, to manufacture vegetable matter in the presence of light. These plants in turn form the base of the food chain in the salt marsh. For example, a phytoplanktonic salad may nourish microscopic zooplankton, the invertebrate organisms that drift in the current. These minute herbivores may then become dinner for predatory zooplankton, which may subsequently become a meal for fish fry, and so on, eventually terminating in the stomach of a heron.

The silence of the marsh is punctuated by the Black-crown's guttural "quock." It has taken flight, beating its wings in strong, measured strokes. It rises above the marsh, circles once, and flies north. For the Black-crown the ascending sun signals the end of the night shift. From the west suddenly appears a flock of seven Snowy Egrets flying in loose formation, each bird holding its neck tightly against its body in an S gesture. The egrets alight on the mudflats and in the tide pools and immediately begin to search for food. Nearby, along a fringe of

OPPOSITE TOP:
Yellow-crowned Night-Herons are specialists at hunting crustaceans by walking slowly and remaining motionless. The breeding range of the Yellow-crown extends from the northeastern United States and Baja California through southeastern Brazil and Peru and includes the Galápagos and West Indian islands.

OPPOSITE BOTTOM:
Black-crowned Night-Herons either stand and wait for their prey or stalk slowly in marshes and on mudflats. Perhaps the most widespread of all herons, the Black-crown occurs from Canada to the southern tip of Argentina, in Africa south of the Sahara, patchily throughout Europe, and continuously across much of Asia to Indonesia. Chincoteague National Wildlife Refuge, Virginia.

Spartina, a Glossy Ibis scours the mud for invertebrate prey, jerkily probing its long, slender, downcurved bill into the soft substrate.

Half a continent to the west, where the sun is still below the horizon, a deep, muffled booming resounds across an inland freshwater marsh—the springtime call of the American Bittern. It has been variously described as a deep, resonant croaking and as resembling the sound produced when a stake is hammered into muddy ground. Consequently, the bittern is known as the stake driver, thunder pumper, mire-drum, and dunk-a-doo. Some have described the call as having a ventriloquial quality, the source being difficult to locate.

The predawn cry of the bittern adds a distinctive tonal richness to freshwater marshes of North America. These marshes, along with bottomland swamps, prairie potholes, wet meadows, bogs, pocosins, and the shores of streams, lakes, and ponds, constitute the most extensive wetland systems on the continent. Fresh water, in fact, flows through almost 95 percent of all wetlands in the continental forty-eight states.

Freshwater marshes often result from a perched, or elevated, water table, which may form a knee-deep basin. These wet areas are quickly colonized by soft-stemmed, water-loving vegetation. Cattails, sedges, and bulrushes stand like green, vertical ribbons along the periphery of a marsh. On gusty days the signature of the wind becomes visible as the verdant stalks sway and bend. In fact, the wind is crucial to these emergent plants because it serves to disperse pollen, and if the

pollen finds a suitable receptacle, to later broadcast the airborne seeds.

Other marshland plants include the distinctive arrowhead, pickerelweed golden club, and the ubiquitous water lily. The particular combination of plants in a freshwater marsh, however, depends on seasonal water levels, water chemistry, and soil type. Besides their botanical inventory, freshwater marshes are home to numerous animals. While myriad insects, such as predacious dragonflies, dart, hover, and zigzag among the aquatic plants, others live a two-dimensional existence on the water's surface. Whirligig beetles spin in dizzying circles as they search for prey, whereas water striders skate in bursts of activity, keeping afloat by virtue of the water's surface-tension properties. Beneath the surface, water boatmen kick their stiff, oarlike legs to propel themselves after likely meals. Nearby, a mosquito fish prowls for its namesake's aquatic larvae, while a newt searches for worms among a bed of freshwater mussels.

All the creatures and plants of a freshwater marsh are intimately and intricately linked together to create the marshland food web. For example, the leaves of a cattail may be munched by insects while its tubers provide a staple for muskrats. The herbivorous insects, in turn, may be eaten by dragonflies, water snakes, or Red-winged Blackbirds, while the portly muskrat may fall prey to mink. The fish that eat mosquito larvae may themselves become dinner for a painted turtle or a snack for an American Bittern. Thus, the life-forms in freshwater marshes exist in dynamic relationships and are indicative of the high productivity of these ecosystems, a productivity that rivals even that of salt marshes.

The enhanced productivity of freshwater marshes rests on the ability of these ecosystems to recycle plant material. Fallen leaves and stems are quickly attacked by armies of invertebrates—snails, larval

Wetlands of Chincoteague National Wildlife Refuge, Virginia.

The painted turtle occurs in sluggish streams and lakes throughout the north, central, and eastern United States.

insects, worms—and later by bacteria, fungi, and hordes of protozoans. Muskrats accelerate the process of decomposition and recycling by gnawing down and shredding great volumes of vegetation in the construction of their lodges. By so doing, the amount of vegetable surface area available to decomposers is significantly increased.

As the accumulated plant material is broken down into ever finer particulate matter, nutrients are leached into the water. These water-borne fertilizers may be absorbed by phytoplankton or by the roots of floating vascular plants. Alternatively, those nutrients that sink into the bottom muck are likely to be pumped out by rooted aquatic vegetation. If the balance between accumulation and decomposition shifts toward the former, bottom sediments begin to amass and ultimately the marsh will fill in and become shallower.

As the sun peeks through the cattails, a bittern ends his imploring song and begins to search for a meal. A solo hunter, the American Bittern is a secretive, elusive denizen of the wetlands, most often glimpsed fortuitously. Sandra McPherson, in the first stanza of her poem "The Bittern," paints an accurate picture of the attitude of a hopeful bittern observer:

> *Because I have turned my head for years*
> *in order to see the bittern*
> *I won't mind not finding*
> *what I am looking for*
> *as long as I know it could be there,*
> *the cover is right,*
> *it would be natural.*

The American Bittern is a chunky, medium-sized member of the family, with an anatomical specialization of the esophagus responsible for producing its booming call. Its plumage is rufous brown above with lighter, streaked underparts. The flight feathers are dark in comparison with the rest of the plumage. A black "mustache" extends along either side of a white throat, at the base of which is a tuft of white feathers that is usually concealed, except during displays. The iris is yellow; the legs, greenish; the bill, yellowish brown. The sexes look alike, and the young appear somewhat similar to the adults.

The preferred habitats of the American Bittern include freshwater marshes with dense vegetation—reeds, cattails, sawgrass—brackish marshes, and wet meadows. In these habitats the bittern finds its favorite prey: fish, insects, crabs, crayfish, reptiles, amphibians—especially frogs—and small mammals such as shrews and voles. To secure this quarry, the bittern waits motionlessly until a potential meal approaches; then, when its victim is within reach, this furtive bird may slowly, almost imperceptibly, sway its neck before striking out with its saberlike bill. A variation of this hunting behavior includes stalking slowly with measured, deliberate steps. The slow movements of the American Bittern have inspired its species name—*lentiginosus*—which shares a common etymology with the musicological term *lentissimo*, meaning in a very slow manner.

When alarmed the bittern emits a "kok-kok-kok" or a deep, nasal call. If the threat is formidable, the bird will point its bill upward in the "bittern posture" and freeze. In doing so, the streaked pattern of its neck blends with a background of dead reeds, rendering the bird virtually invisible. While in this stance, the bittern's eyes bulge outward to enable the bird to look forward. This unusual ability permits binocular vision and the perception of distance so that, if a predator continues to approach, the bittern can flee at the last moment.

As the American Bittern moves stealthily through the freshwater marsh vegetation, seizing those whirligig beetles and mosquito fish unfortunate enough to cross its path, a rustling in the cattails betrays the presence of its tiny cousin, the Least Bittern. This raillike bird is North America's tiniest heron, measuring only thirty centimeters from bill tip to end of tail. Its plumage pattern becomes discernible when the bittern takes flight: wing extremities are dark slate, inner wings are buff and chestnut, and the back and crown (of the male) are greenish black. Two white streaks run laterally down the back, and the underparts are buff with pale streaks. The bill is yellow and green, the iris yellow, and the legs yellow with a dark blush on the front. Differences in plumage between the sexes, which are rare in herons, appear in the Least Bittern in that the female is not as boldly patterned as the male. Also, geographic variation in plumage color is typical of this species, with one form in particular having a dark chestnut plumage.

The Least Bittern is found primarily in freshwater habitats with dense emergent vegetation, such as in this freshwater marsh. Brackish

LEFT:
The Least Bittern (*Ixobrychus exilis*) is recognized by its small size (approximately thirty centimeters), green, brown, and buff plumage, and yellow iris, legs, and feet. The male, as shown here, has a greenish black crown and back.

TOP:
A Least Bittern, the smallest of North American herons, in Eco Pond, Everglades National Park. This diminutive heron is able to slip secretly between reeds by laterally compressing its body.

ABOVE:
The female Least Bittern has a duller plumage than the male. Among herons, Least Bitterns show the greatest difference in plumage between sexes.

ABOVE:
Least Bitterns are furtive and not easily seen. (Note the dark back of this male.) The breeding distribution of this bittern extends along the Atlantic seaboard—and well inland—from southern Canada through the United States and Central America south through Brazil to northern Argentina. Loxahatchee National Wildlife Refuge, Florida.

RIGHT:
The color markings of the female Least Bittern show a buff back rather than the dark green plumage of the male. Anahuac National Wildlife Refuge, Texas.

water marshes and mangrove swamps are also suitable. When disturbed, the Least Bittern flies a short distance with neck extended and legs dangling, often accompanied by a harsh cry, and then drops down into cover. It also may retreat by walking adroitly through thick vegetation. Or if fleeing is not in order, the bird adopts the "bittern posture," much like its larger cousin, with outstretched neck and skyward-pointing bill. In such a stance the Least Bittern, with its streaked neck, becomes highly camouflaged against a background of vertical reeds.

The bulk of the Least Bittern's diet consists of small surface-feeding fish, such as minnows, which are swallowed headfirst. Insects, like dragonflies and aquatic beetles, crustaceans, amphibians, and even small mammals—mice and shrews—are also taken. One bittern purportedly ate the eggs and chicks of a nearby nesting Yellow-headed Blackbird, while another reputedly devoured its own eggs after they were punctured by a Marsh Wren. One of Audubon's pet Least Bitterns gobbled down a hummingbird that was kept in the same room.

As the sun warms the morning air over the marsh, the bittern clutches the reeds with its feet and crouches with its neck extended, its bill just above the water's surface. Then, as a minnow swims below, the bird slowly sways its neck and jabs swiftly. The strike is on target, and the bittern raises its head with a twitching meal between its mandibles. After swallowing the fish headfirst, the bird moves several feet to another vantage point. Although this bird is using an ambush strategy, bitterns may also stalk their prey by walking slowly. They may even glean insects from leaves or seize them as they buzz by.

On the western shore of the freshwater marsh stands a grove of alders, their fallen branches and arching roots creating a tangled maze

Phragmites, also known as reed grass, is a common plant in freshwater and brackish marshes.

of gray, leafless limbs. Poised on one arm of a snag, scanning the water below, a Green-backed Heron waits to surprise a minnow. To most of us, herons are tall, long-legged, elegant birds with a serpentine neck, and many have delicate plumes streaming from their backs and sometimes from their crowns. However, the Green-backed Heron, one of our most common herons, is anything but elegant. A small, stout, thick-necked bird, the Green-back has departed somewhat from typical heron morphology and, in doing so, illustrates the wonderful diversity within this family of birds.

The Green-backed Heron is about the size of a crow, and in flight may even be mistaken for its ebony distant cousin, although the heron has a longer bill and neck. Unlike other herons, the Green-back often flies with its neck outstretched rather than retracted in an **S** curve. Its plumage is chestnut brown on the sides and back of the neck, metallic greenish on the wings and back, and pale gray on the underside. The crown is greenish black, and the iris and legs are yellow.

The Green-backed Heron is one of the most cosmopolitan of all herons. As a consequence of its broad distribution, thirty distinct geographic subspecies, or races, have been identified for this species. Perhaps the most unusual race occurs on the Galapagos Islands. This form, called the Lava Heron, has a charcoal-gray plumage that matches the color of the lava rocks from which this bird hunts.

For such a widespread bird one would expect a diversity of suitable habitats, and this is indeed the case. Green-backed Herons prefer streams, ponds, lakes, lagoons, and coastal areas such as estuaries and mangrove swamps. As a testament to its habitat preference in Australia, this bird is called the Mangrove Heron in the land-down-under. One common characteristic of all these habitats is the presence of tangles of vegetation and snags on which the herons perch and into which the birds may fly to elude predators. Thus, Green-backs are never far from cover. An interesting exception, however, is seen in the Lava Heron. On the Galapagos archipelago, which is virtually free of predators, the Lava Heron forages dauntlessly in the open along shorelines.

The diet of the Green-backed Heron includes small fishes, both aquatic and terrestrial insects and other invertebrates, and small semi-aquatic vertebrates such as frogs. Audubon pictorially depicted a young Green-back reaching for a luna moth. As solitary foragers, these herons typically feed by either walking slowly or, more commonly, by using a stand-and-wait strategy in which the heron perches motionlessly and ambushes approaching prey. Snags and mangrove roots are often used as perches from which the heron crouches and leans forward, craning its neck, its bill almost touching the water. Then, when a minnow, for example, swims within reach, the heron thrusts its head forward, snatches the prey crosswise in its bill, tosses it back, and then swallows the morsel. I once observed an overzealous heron lunge with such force

OPPOSITE TOP:
The Green-backed Heron (*Butorides striatus*) is a small (forty- to fifty-centimeter) heron with a dark green back, buff chest, blackish yellow bill, and yellow iris and legs. Anhinga Trail, Everglades National Park, Florida.

OPPOSITE BOTTOM:
The Green-backed Heron usually feeds by perching in a crouched posture on branches or reeds and jabbing at aquatic prey.

ABOVE:
Besides capturing fish in typical heron fashion, some Green-backed Herons have been observed using bread crumbs and even insects as bait. Merritt Island National Wildlife Refuge, Florida.

LEFT:
One of the most widespread of all herons, the Green-backed Heron occurs in North America from southern Canada throughout most of the United States and south into Mexico. It is also found in Central and South America, Africa south of the Sahara, Asia, and Australia. As a consequence of its broad distribution, the Greenback appears in a variety of geographic subspecies, or races. This relatively small individual is in Loxahatchee National Wildlife Refuge, Florida.

that the bird abandoned its perch and plunged headlong into the water.

In southern Japan Green-backed Herons have been observed bait fishing. Bread crumbs, bits of discarded crackers, insects, berries, and twigs are collected by herons and then dropped onto the surface of a fish pond. This method apparently attracts fish because bait-fishing herons have a better catch success than their non-bait-fishing neighbors. Green-backs will even trim down twigs to form suitable lures and thus are actually modifying and using a tool. At the Miami Seaquarium herons used discarded dry fish pellets that visitors purchased from vending machines. After dropping the bait into the water, the herons would capture fish lured to the bait. If the bait drifted out of striking range, a bird would retrieve it and release it closer. In an even more impressive display of angling finesse, a Green-backed Heron at the Ouachita River in Arkansas was observed capturing live mayflies and using them as living fish lures by placing the insects on the water's surface.

Other observed feeding behaviors include head swaying, foot stirring—presumably to stir up prey in the water—plunging, and swimming. In Africa a Green-back was observed standing in the middle of a stream with its bill pointing upward—the bittern posture—and capturing dragonflies that approached, or landed on, its bill! Occasionally Green-backed Herons become a problem at fish hatcheries by depleting the stock of fish fry. In one instance an entire local population of nuisance Green-backs was mist-netted and successfully relocated to an area where the poachers could cause no mischief.

As the sun mounts higher above the freshwater marsh and the lily pads glisten, the Green-backed Heron remains intent in its silent vigil. The heron's survival depends on the richness of life that moves in many forms through the clear water. The heron's prey, in turn, are sustained by yet other marshland creatures. Ultimately, all life in the marsh, whether animal or vegetable, relies on the presence of pure water—an issue of the clouds and underground streams. Inland freshwater marshes may be no larger than a kiddie pool, but regardless of size, each is a world teeming with a diversity of life-forms.

Whereas inland freshwater marshes typically occur as pockets of water distributed across North America, especially in the northern Midwest and south-central Canada where myriad small ponds carved out by retreating glaciers pockmark the landscape, some of the most expansive freshwater wetlands are found in association with coastal regions. The coastal backwaters of the Mississippi River, for example, inundate thousands of acres in Louisiana, are influenced by the rhythm of tides, and are home to numerous wading birds and other wildlife. One celebrated avian inhabitant of tidal freshwater marshes is the Tricolored Heron. This sleek and impressive bird is perhaps one of the most exquisite herons in the world. In fact, the beauty of this bird

OPPOSITE TOP AND BOTTOM:
The identification of Least Bitterns and Green-backed Herons is sometimes confusing in the field. However, they can be distinguished by body size and bill color.

OVERLEAF PAGES:
Sunrise on Lake Fausse Point in the Atchafalaya Basin, which is part of the Mississippi River delta, and creates the Louisiana bayous. (Photograph by Joan Niemeyer.)

A cypress swamp in the Atchafalaya Basin.

OPPOSITE TOP:
The Tricolored Heron inhabits mainly coastal wetlands from New England to Texas, and south into northern South America. Peapatch Island, Delaware.

OPPOSITE BOTTOM:
Because it is particularly common in the southeastern United States, the Tricolored Heron is also known as the Louisiana Heron. Pea Island, North Carolina.

caught Audubon's eye in 1832, and he described it as "delicate in form, beautiful in plumage, and graceful in its movements." To artist, ornithologist, and birdwatcher alike, few birds measure up to the aesthetic standard established by this species.

The Tricolored Heron is a medium-sized, slender heron with a long, daggerlike bill. Its bluish gray upperparts contrast sharply with its white abdomen, rump, chin, throat, and underwings. Splashes of chestnut occur here and there on its back and at the base of its neck. Its legs are yellow as is its bill, except for the dark tip; its iris is red. In its breeding splendor the Tricolored develops ornamental plumes at the back of its head, the bill becomes deep sky-blue with a jet-black tip, and the leg color intensifies, turning bright orange in some birds. Juveniles resemble adults but have a rufous head and neck and a yellow iris.

The Tricolored is especially abundant in the southeastern United States, thus its original name: Louisiana Heron. This adaptable bird prefers freshwater habitats with shallows, such as marshes and creeks, but is also found in brackish water environments, including mangrove swamps and mudflats. Its diet consists mainly of fish and small invertebrates—insects, crustaceans, and leeches—but it will not hesitate to seize other prey such as frogs and lizards. One bird in Florida was found

The Tricolored Heron (*Egretta tricolor*) is a medium-sized (approximately sixty-five-centimeter), slender heron with blue-gray plumage, white underside, red iris, and yellow bill, legs, and feet.

Tricolored Herons are solitary foragers and vigorously defend feeding territories. Padre Island, Texas.

Tricolored Herons are active hunters and often walk quickly, run, or even dance with raised wings in pursuit of prey.

to have the remains of about two hundred grasshoppers in its gut and must have been foraging on dry turf.

Although Tricoloreds are highly colonial nesters, they are solitary foragers. A hunting bird will not tolerate the presence of other Tricoloreds in its vicinity. Should an intruder approach too closely, the territory-holder will jump with flailing wings at the interloper while emitting a harsh "aah." Such a display is usually enough to send the trespasser on his way.

Like Reddish and Snowy Egrets, Tricolored Herons are active hunters. It is not unusual for these herons to walk quickly or run after a potential meal. They may even leap about with raised wings, turn abruptly, stab at the water with their slender bill, or perform a pirouette while holding a wing extended. On the other hand, Tricoloreds may

As in many herons, the immature Tricolored has a different plumage from that of the adult. Loxahatchee National Wildlife Refuge, Florida.

Immature Tricolored Herons have a yellow iris, which turns red as the birds become adults. These three are in the rookery at Peapatch Island, Delaware.

Besides using active hunting techniques, Tricolored Herons may wait patiently, peering into the water for a potential meal.

Bald cypress and duckweed characterize deep-water forested wetlands in the southern United States.

crouch motionlessly, their neck retracted tightly against their shoulders, and strike almost horizontally at aquatic prey. In contrast, Little Blue Herons typically jab vertically. Tricoloreds are also known for their penchant to wade belly-deep in water. Other feeding behaviors include foot stirring to disturb prey into movement and hovering to capture prey while on the wing.

In the backwaters of the Mississippi River, one of the principal delicacies of herons and humans alike is the ubiquitous "crawfish," a freshwater cousin of the lobster. Tricolored Herons relish these ten-legged crustaceans and can often be seen stalking them in shallow pools. Nearby, a Yellow-crowned Night-Heron, another crayfish connoisseur, may be dozing in a thicket of vegetation, oblivious to the world until its internal alarm clock sounds at dusk. Similarly, a bull alligator may lie motionless, almost completely submerged except for

its eye ridges and the tip of its snout, which protrude through a film of duckweed like miniature volcanic islands.

　　The Mississippi River flows into and mixes with the saline water of the Gulf of Mexico. Besides the Mississippi, numerous other rivers, such as the Atchafalaya, flow into the Gulf and form an almost continuous margin of intracoastal wetlands from Ol' Man River to the Rio Grande. The Intracoastal Waterway is a mosaic of barrier islands, narrow inlets, and sheltered brackish water bays. It is within this network of land and water that the most animated of wading birds, the Reddish Egret, displays its antics.

　　The Reddish Egret is an intermediate-sized member of the heron family with slate-gray plumage and a reddish brown head and neck, the precise colors of which vary geographically. Its bicolored bill (only in adults) is pink with a conspicuous black tip; its legs are cobalt blue; its

By manufacturing vegetable matter in the presence of light, algae form the base of food chains in wetlands across North America.

iris, white, although it appears pale blue in the field. The neck feathers have a shaggy appearance, which is accentuated in the breeding season. The nuptial plumage also exhibits lanceolate plumes on the head and neck.

The Reddish Egret occurs in both dark and white forms, or morphs. Audubon mistakenly believed that the birds "as white as driven snow" were immatures, as are juvenile Little Blue Herons. In another case of mistaken identity, ornithologist Charles L. Bonaparte in 1828 christened the white morph "Peale's Egret" in honor of a Philadelphian naturalist. In the United States about 10 percent of the Texas population and up to 20 percent of those egrets nesting in Florida are of the white morph. (These proportions were likely higher before the slaughter by the plume trade in the late 1800s.) In the Bahamas almost 90 percent of the Reddish Egrets are white-plumed, which throws into question the appropriateness of this bird's common name. In addition, it is not unusual in some localities to observe dark-plumed birds with scattered white feathers or white birds with dark feathers in their wings.

According to Richard Paul, manager of Tampa Bay Sanctuary for the National Audubon Society, the white morph is probably the

The Reddish Egret inhabits shallow, saltwater wetlands along the Florida and Gulf coasts south to Belize and from Baja California to northern South America; it also nests on some West Indian islands, such as Cuba and Hispaniola. This species is dimorphic in that both red and white morphs occur.

OPPOSITE:
The Reddish Egret (*Egretta rufescens*) is a medium-sized (seventy- to eighty-centimeter) egret with blue-gray plumage, a pink bill with a black tip, slate-colored legs, and clear eyes. Merritt Island National Wildlife Refuge, Florida.

Dimorphic genes show in this Reddish Egret. It is sometimes confused with the Little Blue Heron and can be identified by its pink bill. Aransas Bay, Texas.

In the United States from 10 to 20 percent of Reddish Egrets occur in the white morph. In the Bahamas, however, almost 90 percent of these birds are white-plumed. Laguna Madre, Texas.

The "teddi" coloration—designated as such by Lucian Niemeyer in gratitude to Ted Appell, who helped locate the birds—appears only in adult Reddish Egrets. It is unknown from which color morph the mixed-plumed birds develop. White birds may have dark patches, while dark forms may have white splotches in their plumage. Dead Man's Island, Aransas Bay, Texas.

White Reddish Egret engaging in active feeding behaviors. Leaping, running, and turning abruptly with extended wings are some techniques used by these birds to capture fish and other small aquatic creatures.

expression of recessive genes. As a result, all the progeny of a white pair are white. The young of two dark birds are typically reddish, although occasionally a white bird turns up in a brood. When a white and a dark bird mate, both white and dark chicks result. The two-toned coloration has been observed only in adult birds; it is uncertain which color morph the particolored birds develop from. According to Paul's observations, when only a small proportion of white birds are present in a colony, the white individuals breed with dark-plumaged birds. However, when white morphs have a greater representation, say 15 percent of the colony, then the snow-colored birds preferentially mate with like–color morphs.

The Reddish Egret strictly inhabits coastal saltwater environments. Tidal flats, mangrove swamps, and shallow bays are suitable dwellings for this bird. In these habitats egrets locate their favored prey—fish—as well as shrimp and other small aquatic creatures. Reddish Egrets also frequent adjacent freshwater areas where they are likely to capture frogs and tadpoles.

To hunt their prey, Reddish Egrets engage in active, almost frenetic, feeding behaviors, typically leaping and bounding with open wings, turning abruptly, and jabbing at submerged prey. Open-wing feeding—when a bird momentarily extends a wing to create a shadow on the water, presumably to attract fish—slow walking, and foot raking—to stir up bottom-dwelling prey—are additional behaviors used by foraging egrets. While standing still, an egret will often face into the wind and tilt its head as it peers into the water. Although a Reddish Egret may appear preoccupied with its search for food, a neighboring egret that approaches too closely will not go unnoticed. With flailing

A Reddish Egret in breeding plumage in a rookery in Aransas Bay, Texas.

During courtship the Reddish Egret flaunts his shaggy neck feathers. Aransas Bay, Texas.

In about six weeks after hatching, young Reddish Egrets attempt flight; in another three weeks, the grayish brown juveniles are fully fledged and on their own. Aransas Bay, Texas.

Spartina marshes fringe both Atlantic and Pacific coasts of North America and are some of the most productive ecosystems on earth. Bombay Hook National Wildlife Refuge, Delaware.

wings and harsh cries, the hunt will be temporarily abandoned in favor of a vigorous defense of the feeding territory.

In my observations of foraging Reddish Egrets in the shallow shoals of Florida Bay and in mangrove estuaries in northern Mexico, I have noted that hunting often occurs in water that is tarsal-deep, that is, up to the ankles. At this depth, when walking slowly, an egret will raise a foot completely out of the water with each step. In fact, I have at times been close enough to a bird to hear the splash as it placed its foot down.

Although egrets often stand still or turn in one spot, they typically interrupt these stationary stances by walking quickly from site to site. During these movements the egrets sometimes stride almost sideways with their wings extended. When a bird stops, it may stab several times at the water, creating a considerable splash. By walking

in this manner, Reddish Egrets repeatedly traverse a given foraging territory.

When compared with other herons and egrets, the foraging behavior of the Reddish Egret is not only one of the most diversified, but it also includes some of the most elaborate movements and postures. Whereas Snowy Egrets and Tricolored and Little Blue Herons occasionally use open-wing feeding, Reddish Egrets employ this method frequently. Reddish Egrets also go several steps further by often holding both wings extended for long periods, so-called double-wing feeding. This posture presumably reduces glare from glistening surface waters and may serve to attract prey. The Black Heron of Africa, however, surpasses this behavior by actually forming a closed, umbrella-like canopy with its wings. Thus, according to biologist Andrew J. Meyerriecks, one can trace an evolutionary sequence of foraging

Phragmites mostly spreads by rhizomes and can form dense, almost impenetrable stands.

behaviors among the herons culminating in those of the Black Heron, with the Reddish Egret not far behind.

The hunting behaviors, foraging habitats, and prey types of a wading bird constitute, in part, its role in nature—its ecological niche. By definition the respective ecological niches of North American wading birds are not identical, but, as we have seen, many overlap to some degree in habitat use and diet. It is of interest to ecologists to determine just how much overlap occurs between species, because where

Although most often found in upland areas, the gray fox, such as this one in Murrels Inlet, South Carolina, is a predator in some wetlands.

The Osprey feeds almost exclusively on fish in wetlands throughout North America. Flamingo, Everglades National Park, Florida.

The bald cypress is a deciduous conifer and thus sheds its needles for a part of the year. Okefenokee Swamp, Georgia.

overlap occurs competition may result. One reason a given species cannot presumably increase its population indefinitely is because its niche will "press" against niches of species with similar requirements and thus competition will serve to limit its population size. However, what happens when there are no species with which to compete? Under most conditions this question is moot. In the late 1800s, however, a natural experiment was begun that created this very situation. Because the main character was a member of the heron family, its story deserves elaboration.

The Cattle Egret often feeds in the company of large herbivores that inadvertently stir up insects for the attending birds.

We'll never know precisely when, where, or how, but sometime in the late nineteenth century a number of Cattle Egrets ventured a transatlantic crossing from Africa, or possibly southern Europe, to South America. It is not uncommon for birds of the heron family to now and then turn up on shores far from their homes. In 1983 a Western Reef-Heron crossed the Atlantic to Nantucket Island, and as recently as 1990 and 1991, Little Egrets of the Old World were sighted in Nova Scotia. But what makes the Cattle Egret episode unique among herons, indeed unique among birds, is that the original globe-trotters not only remained, they formed the core of what was to become a staggering two-continent colonization. No other vertebrate has undergone such a large-scale, unassisted range expansion during modern times. The Cattle Egret's establishment in the New World has been so successful that in North America its numbers exceed those of all other endemic herons combined!

The Cattle Egret's unassuming appearance belies its history of expansion. It is a medium-sized egret with shorter legs and a thicker neck than other members of the heron family of similar stature. The plumage is typically snow-white, sometimes with a splash of rust here and there, although some birds may have an overall copper appearance; the stout bill is yellow, as are the legs, feet, and iris. During the courtship season, however, the adults appear in brilliant nuptial splendor: the crown, nape, lower neck, and back turn a striking orange-buff color, while the bare areas, including the bill and legs, flush a bright scarlet. When at rest, the Cattle Egret often retracts its neck and assumes a hunched posture similar to that of our night-herons.

In their native homeland Cattle Egrets exist in close association with large ungulates, especially the African Cape buffalo. Unlike most other egrets and herons, Cattle Egrets hunt almost exclusively on land, often side by side with grazing mammals whose movements inadvertently stir up insects for the birds to consume. Besides the Cape buffalo, likely hosts include elephant, rhinoceros, zebra, giraffe, hippopotamus, wildebeest, eland, and waterbuck.

An egret will typically follow, or walk alongside, its host by moving in a fluid, swaggering gait, often with its neck outstretched. As insects, particularly grasshoppers, are flushed from cover, the egret will lunge to grasp its prey. Sometimes a bird will stand and wait for an intended victim, and during those times rhythmic neck swaying is common. Although the Cattle Egret characteristically forages in a loose grouping of birds and pays little attention to neighbors, individual birds have been observed to display threateningly toward others, presumably in defense of their mobile feeding site.

Although grasshoppers constitute their main diet item, Cattle Egrets are opportunistic feeders and take a broad range of prey from beetles and moths to frogs and snakes, and even nestlings of small birds. Because egrets often perch on the backs of their hosts, they may

OPPOSITE:
The Cattle Egret (*Bubulcus ibis*) is a medium-sized (approximately fifty-centimeter) egret with white plumage highlighted by buff when breeding, and yellow bill, legs, and feet, all of which turn red in the breeding season. Loxahatchee National Wildlife Refuge, Florida.

A Cattle Egret in copper plumage is a rare sight. It's not known whether birds with this coloration are unique forms (morphs) or only passing through a particular color phase (age-related) during their maturation. Near Titusville, Florida.

In the late nineteenth century the Cattle Egret expanded its range from Africa into the New World. The earlier introduction of cattle into the Americas, as well as extensive deforestation, created a niche for this opportunistic bird.

A Cattle Egret in copper plumage shows rusty-colored upperparts, a richly colored crest, and a pale underside.

Although an immigrant, the Cattle Egret currently outnumbers all other North American members of the heron family. Besides North America, the Cattle Egret is found throughout Africa—its original home—and in Central and South America, parts of Europe, India, Southeast Asia, and Australia. This bird is in full breeding plumage.

The golden club, an emergent perennial, adds beauty to coastal freshwater wetlands. Okefenokee Swamp, Florida.

by chance discover an engorged tick, which they instantly snatch up. Some observers argue that this deticking is done frequently and deliberately. Regardless, whenever a tick is removed, the egret is performing a service to its host, so their relationship can be thought of as mutually beneficial.

From the foregoing, the ecological niche of the Cattle Egret in its homeland can be summarized as that of an opportunistic feeder, with a concentration on insects, which forages in loose groups, often in the company of grazing mammals in grasslands. How has its particular role in nature enabled this bird to colonize foreign continents and expand so dramatically?

First of all, there is the problem of overcoming a vast, inhospitable geographic barrier: the Atlantic Ocean. Herons in general are capable of sustained long-distance flights as evidenced in extensive postbreeding dispersals and seasonal migrations. Cattle Egrets, in fact, have been regularly observed on such remote oceanic islands as St. Helena and Tristan da Cunha in the Atlantic Ocean, which lie, respectively, eighteen hundred and twenty-eight hundred kilometers from the African mainland. The shortest distance between Africa and South America, measured from the bulge of West Africa to Brazil, is twenty-eight hundred kilometers. Thus, it is certainly plausible that Cattle Egrets have crossed the Atlantic, even repeatedly, especially with the assistance of the prevailing trade winds. But once on the new continent, what explains their astounding success at colonization? And why has colonization occurred only relatively recently? To address these questions, we have to look not only at the Cattle Egret's ecological niche but also at the effect of humans on the landscape.

Since the turn of the century, deforestation in the Americas has accelerated substantially, especially during the past fifty years. What were once unbroken forests in some regions are today isolated fragments engulfed by pastures, cultivated fields, and human settlements. Many of the recently developed, large-scale agricultural systems rely on routine intensive irrigation, which artificially elevates soil moisture content. This, in combination with an almost endless supply of palatable plants, has sustained an explosive herbivorous insect population, which in turn can support the egrets.

Man also altered the New World landscape by introducing herds of domestic livestock four centuries ago. Previous to those introductions, there were no large concentrations of ungulates in habitats suitable to Cattle Egrets. Therefore, from the Cattle Egret's point of view, the periodically flooded croplands, presence of ungulate hosts and abundant prey, and absence of competitors signaled an open invitation to a land that, for all practical purposes, resembled home. By modifying the landscape, man created a "vacant" niche that seemed made to order for occupation by the white-plumed immigrant. Although it is likely that egrets have in earlier times repeatedly arrived in South America from Africa, only recently has there been an ecological niche to accommodate this species.

Today the Cattle Egret is a conspicuous element of the avifauna in the lands it has colonized. Virtually every herd of cattle I have seen in Central America has had its share of attending egrets. It has been estimated that by associating with cattle, foraging egrets increase their prey capture rate by 50 percent while expending only two-thirds the energy as when hunting alone. On many farmlands the tractor has become a rewarding substitute for cattle. Egrets can be seen by the dozens following in the wake of a plow, seizing exposed prey.

Ironically, the Cattle Egret is the most abundant member of the heron family in North America, yet it is the one least prone to hunting in wetlands, although it does feed in wet meadows. All of its egret and heron cousins, however, are intimately linked to places where water meets land. And those places come to fullest expression through the splendor of their aquatic birds. The harmony between wading birds and wetlands is perhaps most clearly seen, felt, and understood in North America's premier wetland ecosystem: the Florida Everglades.

The Seminoles call it *Pa-Hay-Okee,* "grassy waters," the freshwater marshland that spreads over one hundred sixty kilometers southward from Lake Okeechobee to Florida Bay. The underlying limestone riverbed slopes only about three centimeters to the kilometer; thus, the eighty-kilometer-wide sheet of water flows at a snail's pace through sawgrass prairie. As far as the eye can see, the yellowish green carpet of sawgrass stretches beneath the dazzling blue subtropical sky. As the eye scans the prairie, it longs for some topographic irregularity to punctuate and give definition to the monotonous river of grass. These distinctions do, in fact, appear, for where the land rises only thirty to sixty centimeters above the plain, hardwood islands, called hammocks, stand out as do craters on the moon. These hammocks support a unique web of life whose ecological threads reach out to the surrounding wetlands.

Other distinctive features of the glades are found where channels of greater water depth bisect the prairie. These so-called sloughs support a diversity of freshwater plants and large concentrations of wildlife, especially wading birds. However, it is the nondescript, mosslike, floating clumps of mostly algae, called periphyton, that create the circumstances that enable the more familiar species to thrive here. Besides its main ingredients of single-celled algae, the periphyton contains dozens of minute organisms and, as a whole, forms the starting point for numerous food chains in the Everglades. For example, aquatic mosquito larvae and tadpoles feed on the bounty of the floating algal masses; they, in turn, are eaten by small fish, which then are eaten by larger fish, water snakes, turtles, and wading birds, with the food chain terminating in the top carnivore of these freshwater wetlands, the American alligator.

Just as the Everglades ecosystem could not exist were it not for the periphyton floating at the base of the food chain, these magnificent wetlands would be unthinkable without the activities of the alligator basking at the top of the chain. With the approach of the dry season, when a paucity of rain and a scorching sun begin to parch the land, the wetland animals migrate to, and congregate in, water holes dug by these reptilian excavators. The shallow basins, called gator holes, are oases in the temporarily dehydrated landscape and serve as refuges for water-dependent invertebrates, fish, reptiles, and birds. Of course, the alligator does not excavate these reservoirs for altruistic reasons: with the many creatures congregating in its water hole, it has a ready food supply. When the rains return, enough creatures will have escaped the jaws of the alligator to emigrate to safer locales and, once there, to multiply. Thus, predators and prey, plants and herbivores, water and land, form a complex web of interdependencies that constitute the Everglades ecosystem.

Midmorning on the Anhinga Trail, which winds along Taylor Slough in Everglades National Park, can be a propitious time to observe nature. Sawgrass extends from the boardwalk out to the horizon; the margins of each blade of this sedge are rough and jagged, uninviting to the touch. Along a creek grow cattails, pickerelweed, and arrowheads. Like bleached, ghostly fingers, the white petals of spider lily reach into the dawn mist. The leaves and showy flowers of water lilies and spatterdocks define the boundary between water and sky. An alligator glides through the clear water, its body motionless except for the laterally compressed tail that slowly undulates from side to side. As a green treefrog calls in the distance, a quiet splash sounds from nearby. There, in a shallow depression, a white-plumed bird raises its head from the water. Droplets fall from its beak as a struggling salamander squirms between the bird's mandibles. With several jerks of its head, the Snowy Egret swallows its breakfast, then resumes hunting. The egret's stark white plumage set against the green vegetation, both embraced by blue sky, etches an indelible image on the mind's eye.

The Snowy Egret is a medium-sized member of the heron family with pure white plumage and a long, narrow black bill. Its legs are black and contrast sharply with its bright yellow feet, which are often referred to as yellow slippers. Its eyes, too, are yellow. In its breeding regalia, long filamentous plumes, called aigrettes, adorn the Snowy. In the field Snowys may be confused with juvenile Little Blue Herons, the white form of the Reddish Egret, or Cattle Egrets. The Snowy's black bill and legs, however, distinguish this species from the others. Although the plumage of the Great Egret and the "Great White Heron" is similar to that of the Snowy, the former two are much larger and have yellow bills.

The Snowy is typically a diurnal hunter in open wetland habitats, including fresh and brackish water marshes, mangrove swamps, and rivers. Dry grasslands also may provide suitable hunting for Snowys. Their varied diet consists of shrimp, fish, insects, fiddler crabs, small lizards, frogs, snakes, crayfish, and even small mammals.

Snowys have the most diverse repertoire of hunting behaviors among all herons studied. They may employ a stand-and-wait strategy while perched on a snag to ambush aquatic prey, or they may actively pursue potential meals. If the latter strategy is selected, egrets may do

The Snowy Egret (*Egretta thula*) is a medium-sized (fifty-five- to sixty-five-centimeter), white-plumed egret with a black bill, yellow iris, black legs, and yellow feet.

OPPOSITE:
Snowy Egrets use active foraging behaviors, such as walking quickly and wing flicking, when wading in shallow water.

By stirring the water with its yellow feet, this immature Snowy Egret may either be disturbing prey into movement or attracting prey to the brightly colored lure. Merritt Island National Wildlife Refuge, Florida.

The Snowy Egret breeds throughout much of the coastal United States, along both Mexican coasts, in western South America to Chile, and in Argentina. After breeding, northern birds may wander into Canada.

so slowly and steadily, or they may run and jump in an erratic manner. In addition, I have observed Snowys fly above a pond's surface, drag their feet in the water, thrust their heads downward, and then raise their mandibles with a fish twitching between them.

While walking through shallow water, egrets may exhibit wing flicking, where both wings are quickly spread and then folded; open-wing feeding, where one wing is typically outstretched as the egret whirls in a circle; or underwing feeding, where the egret positions its head beneath an extended wing. Ornithologists have been debating the significance of open-wing and underwing feeding. Are they

Loxahatchee National Wildlife Refuge in southern Florida is home to an abundance of wildlife, including many long-legged waders.

By the early twentieth century the Snowy Egret had been hunted almost to extinction in North America to satisfy the demands of the ornamental plume trade. Chincoteague National Wildlife Refuge, Virginia.

adaptations to create a shadow that confuses prey, or shelters to which prey congregate? Or are they behaviors that serve to reduce surface glare?

Foraging Snowy Egrets also make good use of their slippers. While standing in shallows, these birds often agitate the water with one of their feet. This tactic may disturb prey into movement, but it also may actually attract prey to the yellow lure. Similarly, bill vibrating may attract potential quarry.

As a highly colonial species, Snowy Egrets often feed in the company of their own kind and other birds, although they are territorial and will defend an immediate foraging patch. Studies conducted in Panama have shown that models of Snowy Egrets attract Snowys and other avian species to foraging sites, adding credence to the notion that this graceful bird is a core species in feeding aggregations.

By now the Snowy on the Anhinga Trail is satiated. It takes wing and glides a short distance to a snag, where it perches and begins to preen its white cloak. Its ever-versatile bill, at once a spear, nimbly runs down its flight feathers, zippering the fine hooklets along each feather vane. Moreover, the Snowy, like all herons, possesses a comblike middle claw

Members of the heron family use their long bills to zipper up their feathers while preening.

77

The Little Blue Heron (*Egretta caerulea*) is a medium-sized (sixty- to seventy-centimeter), bluish gray heron with a rufous head, black-tipped blue bill, yellow iris, and, in the nonbreeding season, grayish blue legs and feet. Loxahatchee National Wildlife Refuge, Florida.

Little Blue Herons are known in Louisiana as levee-walkers due to their habit of stalking crayfish from levees.

that is used for preening. Specialized feathers—the powder feathers—produce a dustlike down that presumably absorbs and removes fish oils as it is combed into the plumage.

As the white egret grooms, nearby its dark cousin stealthily pursues an aquatic meal. Unlike the quick actions of the Snowy, the Little Blue Heron uses slow, deliberate movements and pauses for long periods to peer at the water. The Little Blue has a slate-bluish gray plumage tinged with maroon on the neck and head; its legs and feet are dull greenish yellow; and its iris is pale yellow, although it can appear light blue under

The Little Blue Heron in breeding plumage has cobalt legs and bill. The Reddish Egret, which is sometimes confused with the Little Blue, is larger and has a pink bill with a black tip.

The Delmarva fox squirrel, a subspecies of fox squirrel originally found in hardwood swamps from southeastern Pennsylvania to the southern tip of Maryland's Delmarva Peninsula, is listed as an endangered species. Due to habitat loss, this mammal is presently restricted to the Delmarva Peninsula and several local sites where it has been released.

field conditions. Its bill is two-toned—grayish blue at the base, black at the tip—and stouter than the bills of similarly sized herons. During courtship and breeding the lores become a deep sky-blue, the legs darken, lanceolate plumes develop on the nape and back, and the head and neck become redder. Although this is an accurate description, if one were to rely on only these field marks, many Little Blues would be overlooked! The reason, of course, is that juveniles have a markedly different appearance. Unlike the blue adults, the young sport a pure white plumage until their second year. In addition, the juveniles have yellower eyes.

The white plumage of an immature Little Blue Heron is strikingly different from that of the adult. Ding Darling National Wildlife Refuge, Florida.

In its second year the young Little Blue Heron molts its white feathers and assumes the blue garb of the adult. Loxahatchee National Wildlife Refuge, Florida.

Plumage dimorphism (color differences between adult individuals of the same species) is not uncommon in herons. Reddish Egrets, as we have seen, occur in both dark and white morphs, and the Great Blue Heron has a white form found mainly in the Florida Keys. Moreover, such dimorphism is not restricted to herons, for both the Snow Goose and Ross' Goose, for instance, occur in blue and white morphs, and Screech Owls can be rusty or gray.

What distinguishes the Little Blue Heron from the aforementioned birds is that its juvenile plumage is so strikingly different from that of the adult. Although many birds, including herons, undergo color changes from youth to maturity, few are as dramatic as that seen in the phases of the Little Blue. A notable exception is the White Ibis, whose snow-white adult plumage contrasts sharply with the soft browns of juveniles. Just why the Little Blue exhibits such a marked difference in plumage between ages is puzzling. It is interesting that another heron, the Pied Heron of northern Australia, undergoes a transformation from a white juvenile plumage to a dark slate-colored adult plumage, but the change is restricted only to the feathers of the

The Little Blue Heron often waits patiently for prey to approach and then jabs vertically downward with its bill.

Because their diet often includes large amounts of fish, which can easily soil their plumage, members of the heron family spend much time grooming. A specialized comblike toe and powder down feathers facilitate grooming.

The heron family (Ardeidae) contains about sixty species worldwide, which are typically characterized by long legs, a long neck, and a saberlike bill.

Little Blue Herons nest colonially alongside other herons, egrets, and other wetland birds. Peapatch Island, Delaware.

The Little Blue Heron breeds along the Atlantic and Gulf coasts but disperses well inland when the breeding season is over. It also nests on the southern tip of Baja and along both Mexican coasts through Central and South America.

face, crown, and crest. In Magnificent Frigatebirds, too, the juveniles are white-headed while the adults have glossy black heads. Aside from their different plumages, adult and juvenile Little Blues show no significant behavioral differences, although immatures are somewhat less efficient at hunting.

The habitat preference of the Little Blue Heron is varied and includes a diversity of freshwater inland areas. Marshes, lagoons, and shallow wetlands are typical habitats. Flooded and dry grasslands and even marine coasts, especially when associated with islands, are also frequented. In Louisiana, Little Blues are often encountered in rice fields, where they walk along levees to hunt crayfish, earning them the local name, levee-walkers.

The Little Blue's diet consists of crustaceans such as crayfish and fiddler crabs, other small invertebrates, fish, small reptiles, and frogs. To locate these prey, herons slowly and methodically patrol an area, often retracing their previous steps. In addition to walking slowly, Little Blues may stand motionless, stretching their necks and peering into the water, or they may rake the substrate with a foot, presumably to disturb prey into movement. They may occasionally walk quickly, or even run, but these energetic behaviors are more typical of similarly sized Snowy Egrets and Tricolored Herons.

Little Blue Herons have been observed feeding with Cattle Egrets in fields and in association with White Ibises. When in the company of ibises, Little Blues double the number of prey captures compared with solitary foraging herons. Apparently, ibises unintentionally stir up food as they walk, thereby increasing the number of prey available to nearby Little Blues. In exchange the herons may serve as sentinels to alert the ibises to danger. Not all associations between wading birds, however, are mutually beneficial or even peaceable. Little Blues and other wading birds occasionally have their captured prey stolen by a notorious robber, the Great Egret.

The Great Egret, which has also been known as American Egret, Common Egret, and Great White Egret, is North America's second tallest heron species, following the Great Blue Heron. It sports an immaculate white plumage, which contrasts sharply with the dark, almost black, legs. Its bill is usually yellow with a black tip, being

In contrast to the active feeding behaviors of similarly sized herons and egrets, the Little Blue hunts slowly and often peers into the water for long periods of time. Fish and other small prey constitute the Little Blue's diet.

CLOCKWISE FROM TOP LEFT:
The Hudson River floodplain. Bear Mountain State Park, New York.

The sika deer, a native of Asia, has been introduced in Maryland and is now feral in Chincoteague National Wildlife Refuge, Virginia. Although they prefer forested areas, these deer find marshes suitable habitat.

The bullfrog is a common amphibian of freshwater wetlands and may fall prey to the Great Blue Heron and other large species of wading birds. Bombay Hook National Wildlife Refuge, Delaware.

An early morning sun illuminates the Louisiana bayous of the Atchafalaya Basin. Lake Fausse Point, Louisiana.

somewhat darker in juveniles; its lores and iris are yellow. An exaggerated crook in its neck is conspicuous when the egret is standing upright. The breeding dress is spectacular: over three dozen lengthy scapular plumes (aigrettes) extend well beyond the tail feathers, the bill color intensifies to orange, and the lores flush green.

The habitat of the Great Egret is varied but typically includes a body of shallow water. Both saline and freshwater marshes, shallow bays, the banks of sluggish streams, mudflats in tidal estuaries, and the fringes of mangrove swamps and lakes are suitable for this bird. In addition, wet meadows, agricultural fields, and drainage ditches offer habitat to this species.

The Great Egret feeds mainly on fish, but as an opportunist like most herons, it will not bypass anything manageable. Consequently, its diet includes insects, crayfish, frogs, salamanders, snakes, small mammals, and occasionally small birds. The mammalian prey, such as mice, are most often captured in terrestrial habitats.

The hunting behavior of the Great Egret epitomizes patience. Standing motionless in shallow water with its head and neck held at a forty-five-degree angle to the water's surface, or taking several slow, deliberate steps while craning its neck are its two most frequently

The Great Egret (*Casmerodius albus*) is a large (ninety-five- to one-hundred-centimeter), white-plumed egret with yellow bill and iris and black legs and feet. The yellow lores turn bright green in the breeding season. Chincoteague National Wildlife Refuge, Virginia.

The long, pointed bill of the Great Egret enables this wader to capture fish, crayfish, frogs, and a host of other small creatures. In most members of the heron family, the bill is slightly serrated to facilitate grasping slippery, struggling prey.

observed foraging behaviors. When a potential meal is discovered, the egret will slightly retract its neck, then strike almost directly downward with lightning speed. As in other members of the heron family, the quickness of the strike is attributed to specialized cervical vertebrae and muscles, which give the neck its characteristic kink. Fish are swallowed headfirst after a brief manipulation between the mandibles. One study showed that about three out of four strikes successfully procure a meal. Besides these more typical feeding behaviors, Great Egrets, like their Cattle Egret cousins, have been observed capturing insects stirred up by grazing cattle.

Great Egrets may feed solitarily or in loose groups of other egrets and other species of wading birds. I have observed Great Egrets feeding in mixed flocks of Wood Storks, Snowy Egrets, and Tricolored Herons in southern Florida. These mixed flocks are usually peaceful, the individual birds disregarding each other; however, as mentioned earlier, instances of prey robbing do occur. Ecologist James Kushlan noted that Great Egrets will rob other egrets, White Ibises, and Little Blue Herons, but no species larger than themselves, such as Wood Storks or Great Blue Herons.

Prey-robbing behavior in Great Egrets poses somewhat of a theo-

retical problem because the time and energy invested in piracy and the resulting reward do not outweigh the energy balance of a nonrobbing egret. In other words, it is not beneficial in terms of energy gain to rob other birds of their catch. So why is prey robbing observed in *Great Egrets* and other species? A study of wading birds off the Panamanian coast offers one plausible explanation. According to researcher Gloria Caldwell, the most important aspect of robbing is the acquisition of the victim's foraging site. An egret that displaces another egret or another species of heron subsequently has a greater foraging success in its new feeding site compared with its previous record. Furthermore, those individual birds whose sites are usurped experience reduced prey capture rates. Thus, the benefit from prey robbing is not in the immediate reward of the pilfered food but in the longer-term access to a better foraging site.

Great Egrets are a common sight in the Florida Everglades. In these vast, freshwater wetlands, wildlife and environment, organism and context constitute two sides of the equation of life. One cannot exist without the other. Similarly, on a grander scale an ecosystem such as the Everglades does not exist in isolation but is intimately connected to neighboring ecosystems. One such ecosystem that borders and

When not hunting, many members of the heron family spend their time in roosts.

OVERLEAF LEFT, TOP:
Due to its large size, the Great Egret is able to wade deeper than smaller herons and egrets.

OVERLEAF LEFT, BOTTOM :
Great Egrets hunt by waiting motionlessly or walking slowly. When a fish, for example, swims within reach, the egret stabs at the water with lightning speed and deadly accuracy.

OVERLEAF RIGHT:
By having their eyes placed on the sides of their head, members of the heron family get a panoramic view of their surroundings, which may save them when predators approach.

blends into the Everglades is known as Big Cypress Swamp, one of North America's southern deep-water swamps.

Within the vast acreage of Big Cypress Swamp lie the National Audubon Society's Corkscrew Swamp Sanctuary and the Fahkahatchee Strand. Like their ecological counterparts—Okefenokee Swamp in northern Florida and southern Georgia, Atchafalaya Swamp in Louisiana, and remnants of Great Dismal Swamp in Virginia and North Carolina—the cypress swamps of southern Florida are places of mystery. Spanish moss, like giant cobwebs, drapes from almost every branch; bromeliads adorn tree trunks; alligators and cottonmouths lurk silently in the shadows by day; and the nocturnal silence is punctuated by the hooting of Barred Owls.

These deep-water forested wetlands are dominated by either bald cypress and water tupelo or pond cypress and black gum, depending on whether the soils are, respectively, nutrient rich or relatively infertile. The standing water is more or less permanent and often covered by a

OPPOSITE TOP:
In the breeding season, the Great Egret develops long aigrettes, its iris color intensifies to red, and its lores turn bright green. Aransas Bay, Texas.

OPPOSITE BOTTOM:
The Great Egret exerts considerable effort to become airborne; Atchafalaya Basin, Louisiana.

The needles of bald cypress add color to southern bottomland hardwood swamps.

A river floodplain of the Congaree River in the Congaree National Wildlife Refuge, South Carolina.

91

green veneer of duckweed and other surface-water plants. Protruding through this verdant film, cypress knees stand like miniature cathedrals in an enchanted kingdom. These knobby outgrowths function like snorkels, helping the underwater roots to breathe. Many of the larger trees sport wide flanges at their base, called buttresses, which may help support the forest giants. The largest cypress trees are not only prodigious in stature but also in age. A typical tree can live for more than five centuries, and one bald cypress in Corkscrew Swamp is estimated to be seven hundred years old.

Cypress swamps typically occur in coastal regions. In fact, their proximity to the coast may be a clue to their origin. Okefenokee Swamp, for example, was presumably formed during the Pleistocene when retreating waters of the Atlantic Ocean became trapped behind a sand ridge. Today, Okefenokee Swamp, which encompasses almost a half-million acres, is an isolated body of water, with the exception of its forming the headwaters of the Suwannee and St. Mary's rivers.

Much of the animal life of cypress swamps is quiescent by day, becoming active only after dusk. Alligators, raccoons, bobcats, and otters nocturnally patrol the wetlands for their respective prey, which ranges from crayfish and snails to frogs and fish. Like wetlands in general, the food chains of a cypress swamp begin with detritus, the accumulation of decaying vegetable matter. This material is cycled through mosquito larvae to fish to otter and then returned to the water, transformed

A Great Egret lifts into the air from the Atchafalaya Basin, Louisiana.

A cypress forest in Middle Fork of the Suwannee River in Okefenokee Swamp, Georgia.

The essence of wetlands comes to fullest expression in their wading birds. Here, a Great Blue Heron graces Okefenokee Swamp in southern Georgia. Billy's Lake, Stephen Foster State Park, Georgia.

through the otter's wastes to provide fertilizer for the vegetation. Thus, materials are cycled and recycled through these wetland ecosystems.

The bird life of cypress swamps is varied and multitiered, ranging from the canopy above to the still waters below. While Pileated Woodpeckers hammer away in the heights, wading birds of many shapes and sizes stalk in the shallows. Perhaps the most statuesque wader in these southern swamps, as well as in northern hardwood

The river otter is found in rivers and still bodies of water throughout Canada and the United States. It feeds mainly on fish, frogs, and crayfish and can remain submerged for several minutes.

The raccoon is a nocturnal mammal found mainly in wooded riparian wetlands across much of North America. As a predator and scavenger, this carnivore preys on the eggs and young of wading birds.

swamps, is the Great Blue Heron, a bird that is itself a living language of the swamp. If I were asked to select one representative species that symbolizes both the essence of the heron family and the wildness of North American wetlands, the Great Blue—one of the best known and most cherished wetland birds across the continent—would undoubtedly be my choice.

The Great Blue Heron, which can live longer than twenty years,

With a wingspan of two meters, a Great Blue Heron labors to take flight. Bombay Hook National Wildlife Refuge, Delaware.

The Great Blue Heron (*Ardea herodias*), the largest North American heron (one hundred five to one hundred twenty-five centimeters), has a bluish gray plumage, yellow bill and iris, and yellowish gray legs.

The range of the Great Blue Heron is the most northerly of all North American herons and reaches into southern Alaska. It is the most widely distributed heron in Canada. Its distribution also covers Central America, the Galápagos, and islands in the Caribbean.

OPPOSITE:
Young Great Blue Herons are not as boldly patterned as adults. The adult plumage is attained after the second year. Galveston Island, Texas.

is the largest heron in North America, standing one hundred twenty centimeters tall with a wingspan exceeding two meters. Its long, serpentine neck and tall, spindly legs give this heron the appearance of being the "giraffe" of birds. The Great Blue Heron has a bluish gray plumage and sports a distinctive white head, crown, and chin with a contrasting black stripe above the eyes, which trails into a black crest. Splashes of rich chestnut adorn the thighs. The bill and iris are yellow, and the legs are a dull, dark yellow. Juveniles resemble adults except the former are more streaked and have a dark crown.

At one time considered to be a separate species, the white race of the Great Blue Heron, the "Great White Heron" (*Ardea herodias occidentalis*), is found mainly in saltwater habitats of southern Florida.

OPPOSITE:
The "Wurdemann's Heron" (*Ardea herodias "wurdemanni"*) is a morph of the Great Blue found in southern Florida. It has a white head and white topknot. Although at one time considered a separate subspecies, this form most likely originated through hybridization between dark and white morphs. No Name Key, Florida.

In southernmost Florida and the Keys, the Great Blue appears in a snow-white guise with greenish or pinkish legs. The "Great White Heron" is not an albino but a race of the Great Blue, which in the past may have been geographically isolated from the dark form. Due to its distinctive plumage, the white form was at one time considered a unique species. However, most behavioral and morphological studies find no significant differences that would warrant separate species status—a distinction that is somewhat arbitrary. To further complicate matters, southern Florida populations of Great Blues may include white morphs (as in Reddish Egrets), which are indistinguishable from individuals of the white subspecies. Although white and blue forms sometimes pair up, producing both white and blue—and occasionally mixed-colored—young in the nest, there is a tendency for blues to mate preferentially with blues and whites with whites.

The "Ward's Heron" of the Gulf coast is another geographic subspecies of Great Blue Heron. It has a white neck, black topknot, and a paler plumage than that of a typical Great Blue. The "Wurdemann's Heron" of the Florida Keys has a white head, white topknot, and bluish body. This morph is not considered a subspecies in that it most likely originated as a hybrid between dark and white forms.

The "Ward's Heron" (*Ardea herodias wardi*) is a subspecies of the Great Blue found from Florida to the Texas coast. It has a white head and a black topknot. Goose Island State Park, Texas.

A wide array of habitats is suitable to Great Blue Herons: freshwater swamps, streams, ponds, lakes, and marshes; saltwater estuaries, bays, mangroves, and mudflats; wet meadows; and dry land such as pastures and agricultural fields. Although as a species the Great Blue Heron is considered a generalist in its habitat preference, the white-plumed subspecies of southern Florida is considered a specialist in its almost exclusive use of saltwater shallows in Florida Bay and associated wetlands.

The Great Blue, like many herons, is an omnivore and an opportunist. Insects, crustaceans, fish, amphibians, reptiles, mammals, and occasionally birds—such as rails—are readily eaten. To capture these prey, Great Blue Herons either stand patiently, waiting to ambush an unsuspecting passerby, or wade slowly. Often a heron will hold its neck outstretched at about a forty-five-degree angle, its eyes peering intently downwards. When prey is discovered, a quick thrust of the spearlike bill usually insures a capture. Other observed foraging behaviors include jumping, running, wing flicking, swimming feeding, and plunging. Not all Great Blues, however, work hard for their dinner; numerous individuals have been known to panhandle from obliging humans.

After prey is secured, the heron will manipulate it in its bill before ingestion. Fish must be swallowed headfirst to insure that their scales won't lodge in the bird's throat. Sometimes, however, herons encounter difficulties. I observed a Great Blue in Florida Bay capture a large pancake-shaped fish, which seemed more than a mouthful. After handling the prize for forty-five minutes, which included dropping it and retrieving it repeatedly, the heron, much to

Life poses difficult challenges to young Great Blue Herons; typically, only three out of ten will survive to adulthood.

An immature Great Blue Heron in late summer molt in Bombay Hook National Wildlife Refuge, Delaware.

my amazement, accomplished the task! However, for another thirty-six minutes, the gratified heron strutted around with a telltale bulge midway in its throat. That individual presumably was fortunate—there are numerous reports of Great Blues choking to death on excessively large fish.

These tall birds are capable of wading to depths inaccessible to other species of waterbirds and can thus exploit a part of a wetland resource that is unused by other species, thereby limiting competition. However, competition may be significant among individual Great Blues, and when prey are scarce and widely dispersed, Great Blue Herons tend to be territorial. Conversely, if their prey are locally concentrated, such as in a drying pond, herons typically feed peaceably in groups.

A study conducted by Range Bayer in Oregon wetlands found that some individual herons occupied their chosen feeding territory for several years. Juveniles were excluded from the prime feeding locations and thus established territories at the periphery of the areas held by the adults. If this exclusion from the better feeding sites is characteristic, it may be partly responsible for the high mortality rates of first-year birds, whereby only three out of ten juveniles survive. Young birds may be further handicapped by being inefficient hunters. A study in Nova Scotia found that juveniles were only about half as successful as adults

Due to their large size and long, spindly legs, Great Blue Herons are able to wade in depths inaccessible to smaller waterbirds. Blackwater National Wildlife Refuge, Maryland.

OPPOSITE TOP:
The Great Blue Heron can use its spearlike bill to impale fish. After capture, the heron will manipulate the fish in its mandibles, then swallow it headfirst. Merritt Island National Wildlife Refuge, Florida.

OPPOSITE BOTTOM:
Immature Great Blue Herons are not as adept as adults at securing food and take time to perfect their hunting skills.

Great Blue Herons are wary birds and will take flight when threatened. Chincoteague National Wildlife Refuge, Virginia.

in the number of prey captures per attempt. Young Great Blues apparently have the odds of survival stacked against them.

The presence of the Great Blue Heron graces wetlands from coast to coast and from Canada to the Gulf of Mexico. In the northern reaches of its range, this adaptable heron may be the only species of wader found in marshes and riparian habitats. In the diverse habitats of southern Florida, however, Great Blues are far from alone because the greatest diversity of wading birds in North America occurs on the tip of the Florida peninsula. And perhaps the most species-rich habitats of this subtropical region are the previously maligned coastal mangrove swamps.

At one time thought to be no more than steamy, mosquito-infested, impenetrable jungles, mangrove swamps have recently enjoyed better public relations as our understanding of their ecological infrastructure has grown. In fact, we now recognize these intertidal forests as vital links between terrestrial and marine ecosystems, themselves supporting myriad life-forms.

Perhaps the best way to explore a mangrove swamp is to glide through one in a canoe. As one paddles quietly through the tangled maze, branches of mangrove trees reach outward like greeting hands

A "Ward's Heron" in breeding plumage on Galveston Island, Texas.

OPPOSITE:
Great Blue Herons are opportunistic feeders and will take any prey that are manageable.

OVERLEAF LEFT:
At least five geographic subspecies of Great Blue Heron have been identified; birds from Galveston Island, Texas, exhibit more pastels and reds than other races.

OVERLEAF RIGHT:
A "Great White Heron," the white form of the Great Blue, in Chincoteague National Wildlife Refuge, Virginia.

with innumerable verdant fingers. Mosquitoes hover mercilessly, waiting for the opportune moment to strike. The cry of a Belted Kingfisher pierces the silence while various species of warblers dart among the leaves, gleaning tiny insects. As the canoe glides farther inland, the water becomes increasingly tea-colored, stained by the tannins of shed mangrove leaves and bark.

Mangrove swamps are the subtropical and tropical equivalents of northern salt marshes, both being characteristic of brackish and saltwater coastlines. The trees for which these swamps are named are the only trees in the world adapted to saline water. Although mangrove trees can exist in fresh water, there they would be out-competed by other species. So, by venturing where other trees dare not go, mangroves have carved out a unique ecological niche.

In southern Florida, mangrove forests occur where fresh water of the Everglades ecosystem drains into the Gulf of Mexico and Florida Bay. The mixing of this fresh water, as well as rain, with the daily influx of seawater brought in by high tides creates the hydrologic circumstances necessary for mangroves to take root. Furthermore, the supply of fresh water has the added advantage of carrying suspended organic matter, which originated inland but is now available to nourish the mangrove ecosystem. Likewise, incoming tides transport nutrients from the sea to the mangrove environment. The mangrove swamp, in turn, exports organic matter to the marine ecosystem. Thus, land and sea are linked in a dynamic interchange via the mangrove forests, again underscoring the fact that ecosystems are intimately interconnected.

The dominant characters of the mangrove swamp are the shrub-

Red mangrove stump in Everglades National Park, Florida, where fresh and salt water mingle.

Mangrove trees, such as these red mangroves in southern Florida, are the only trees in the world capable of growing in saline water. Boggy Key, Florida.

Mangrove trees, such as this thicket of red mangrove on Boggy Key, Everglades National Park, help build up and stabilize shorelines.

like trees, several species of which inhabit the south Florida coast. The one that reaches farthest into the sea and stands on spiderlike legs is the red mangrove. This species has a high tolerance to salt and is found from below the low tide line, where it is continuously submerged, to the intertidal zone, where it is alternately inundated and exposed by daily tides. The black mangrove anchors on higher ground, where it is touched only by high tides, and sends forth an army of rootlike growths that project through the mud like the bristles of a brush. These projections, called pneumatophores, as well as the stilt roots of the red mangrove, are perforated by narrow slits used for gas exchange—adaptations that serve as snorkels for trees rooted in oxygen-poor mud.

Red and black mangroves are found nearest the edge of the sea and presumably serve to stabilize the shoreline, but white mangroves typically predominate at a greater distance from the water. And higher still, in the transition zone between mangroves and upland areas, stand the buttonwood trees, which are in reach of only spring tides and storm surges and are the least tolerant of salt water.

Mangrove trees have various strategies to deal with saline water. Some prevent altogether—or significantly minimize—the uptake of salt by specialized root-cell membranes. Others, like white and especially black mangroves, actively secrete salt through their leaf surfaces, as a lick of a leaf will readily demonstrate. Some trees simply shed their older leaves to periodically remove excess salt concentrations.

The trees of mangrove forests form a structural network in which many animals make their home. Legions of barnacles and oysters cluster on the prop roots of red mangrove, filtering the nutrient-rich waters for their sustenance. When tides withdraw and mudflats appear, hordes of fiddler crabs scuttle to and fro in a bustle of activity. Snails travel along highways of roots, trunks, and branches; while mussels, sponges, and sea squirts cling to roots from which they will never wander. Numerous fish move with ease among the submerged networks, which serve as refuges when danger approaches. And danger may take many forms: a larger fish, a turtle, a saltwater crocodile, or a wading bird.

As in other wetland ecosystems, the food chains of a mangrove swamp originate in the supply of detritus, nutrients washed into the mangrove forest from inland areas and from the sea. These liquid fertilizers provide raw materials for the trees to grow, develop, produce flowers and fruits, and, most importantly, to bring forth an abundant supply of leaves. When these leaves grow old, they drop from their branches and settle in the water where they are soon attacked by bacteria, fungi, and protozoa, which form a film on the discarded foliage, ultimately decomposing them to particulate matter, which is then available to small fish, shrimp, crabs, and other creatures. These detritivores, as they are called, themselves become food for other mangrove inhabitants and yet again the fabric of interdependence is woven in this ecosystem.

Florida redbelly turtles often bask for long periods in ponds and marshes. Adults are mostly herbivorous and do not compete for food with wading birds. Loxahatchee National Wildlife Refuge, Florida.

Rounding a bend in the canoe, a distant mudflat surrounded by tangles of prop roots comes into view. A flock of Snowy Egrets scours the mud and shallow pools for food. Nearby, a dark-plumaged bird unobtrusively goes about its business of hunting by probing its long bill into the mud. Three of the egrets on the flats have moved within a neck's stretch of the dark bird, which is now traversing a shallow tide pool. As it probes erratically into the mud, the sunlight catches its plumage in such a way that the previously dull color takes on a subtle radiance for which this bird, the Glossy Ibis, is named.

The Glossy Ibis belongs to a worldwide family of wading birds that includes other ibises and the spoonbills. The most salient feature of the ibis is its decurved bill, which looks as if it was stretched like putty to an exaggerated length. The bird's plumage, when well illuminated, appears mostly chestnut with a greenish sheen, and its eyes are reddish brown. In flight, with outstretched neck, trailing legs, and long glides, the silhouette of the ibis evokes visions of antediluvian time when pterodactyls roamed the skies.

When feeding, as the ibis swings its head from side to side, the nerve endings in its bill detect any small prey it encounters. Thus, its sense of touch, as well as quick mandibular reflexes, is of paramount

The American alligator is the top predator of the food chain in southeastern wetlands. At one time almost hunted to extinction, this reptile has recovered due to state and federal protection.

Different species of wading birds typically form mixed-species feeding aggregations. Here, in Merritt Island National Wildlife Refuge in Florida, Tricolored Herons, White Ibises, and Roseate Spoonbills feed side by side.

In the breeding season, the plumage of the Glossy Ibis turns chestnut with an iridescent sheen. This species ranges from the north-eastern United States to northern South America and the Greater Antilles. It also occurs in southern Europe, Africa, Asia, and Australia.

value to the ibis. Unlike the egrets, its eyes are of little help in securing meals when foraging in shallow water.

The Glossy Ibis frequents both coastal and inland marshes, fresh-water swamps, and floodlands. It's not unusual for this gregarious bird to fly thirty kilometers from its nightly tree roost to its foraging grounds, where it hunts for crayfish, insects, and small vertebrates such as snakes. Hunting ibises may either walk on mudflats or wade belly-deep in shallows. As an ibis forages for a meal, egrets may be observed in close attendance snatching up any likely morsel disturbed by its movements. Snowy Egrets are known to feed in association with ibises and other species that may inadvertently stir up prey for the oppor-tunistic egrets. As mentioned earlier, studies of Little Blue Herons feeding in association with White Ibises show herons double their food intake when hunting alongside ibises, so presumably these Snowys are enjoying a similar benefit. Does the ibis gain from this association? Supposedly, yes, by profiting from the extra pairs of watchful eyes that could more readily detect a potential predator. Sometimes, however, ibises are negatively influenced by other species close at hand. Grackles, for example, commonly swipe captured prey from foraging ibises.

The Glossy Ibis, which breeds along the eastern shores of the Gulf of Mexico, throughout Florida, and north along the Atlantic

The Glossy Ibis (*Plegadis falcinellus*) is a medium-sized (fifty-five- to sixty-centimeter) wader with a dark, iridescent plumage, which often looks black; a brownish, decurved bill; a brown iris; and dark grayish legs. It is found mostly east of the Mississippi River. Merritt Island National Wildlife Refuge, Florida.

Like other ibises, the Glossy Ibis feeds by probing with its long bill, which has an acute sense of touch. This species may repeatedly visit a favorite foraging area.

The White-faced Ibis (*Plegadis chihi*) is a medium-sized (fifty-five-to sixty-centimeter) wader with a dark plumage with an iridescent sheen; a brown, decurved bill; red eyes and red legs; and, especially in the breeding season, a white facial border. It is found mostly west of the Mississippi River. Padre Island, Texas.

coast, has a look-alike relative west of the Mississippi: the White-faced Ibis. In fact, the two are so similar in appearance and behavior that ornithologists consider them sibling species, or even races of the same species. A breeding White-faced Ibis, however, has a red bill and face surrounded by a white, feathered margin. The White-face's eyes are also redder than those of the Glossy Ibis.

Although the White-face is found in coastal areas, its main populations occur well inland, especially in the Great Basin states, where it hunts in freshwater wetlands such as flooded fields, wet meadows, tule marshes, ponds, and irrigated lands. Consequently, compared to the Glossy Ibis, the White-faced Ibis' diet includes proportionately more insects, earthworms, and leeches, which it captures by probing and gleaning. In addition, frogs, newts, and small fish are taken. In contrast to its look-alike cousin, the White-faced Ibis rarely roosts in trees—piles of well-concealed marsh vegetation and the banks of ponds and streams are the preferred roosting sites.

An early-morning watch over Florida's mangrove swamps is inevitably rewarded with sightings of North America's third species of ibis. Like a string of glowing pearls, a flock of three dozen White Ibises,

Unlike herons, which fly with their necks curved against their bodies, ibises fly with their necks outstretched. This White-faced Ibis is airborne above West Bay, Galveston, Texas.

During the breeding season the White-faced Ibis develops a conspicuous white fringe bordering its face, which gives this bird its common name. This species breeds from western and central United States to central Mexico, and patchily through South America.

The brackish water marshes of Chincoteague National Wildlife Refuge, Virginia, are dominated by *Spartina* grass and serve as nurseries for many species of fish.

ABOVE:
The White-faced Ibis often feeds in the company of other long-legged waders, such as these Roseate Spoonbills.

RIGHT:
Rabbit Key, Florida began as a red mangrove seed.

OPPOSITE:
In flight, the White Ibis displays its black wingtips. Squadrons of White Ibises flying in **V** formation offer impressive sights above southern coastal wetlands.

The White Ibis (*Eudocimus albus*) is a medium-sized (sixty- to sixty-five-centimeter) wader with a pure white plumage, a long, red, decurved bill, a clear iris, and red legs.

The White Ibis typically forages by walking on mudflats or wading in shallow water. The eye reflects the color of the sky. Okefenokee Swamp, Georgia.

flying in a broad **V** formation, appears overhead. In unison the birds bank and veer, as if avoiding an invisible obstacle, and alternately flap and rest their wings. The flock rises and falls as it approaches the mudflats exposed by low tide. With extended necks and trailing legs, their wings tickle the air with an audible swishing sound and reflect the warm colors of the dawn sun.

This impressive aerial choreography of White Ibises did not go unnoticed by eighteenth-century explorer William Bartram. In his *Travels* (1792) he wrote:

Immature White Ibises sport a brown plumage with white under-parts. Everglades National Park, Florida.

In breeding condition, the legs and bill of the White Ibis are brilliant scarlet.

It is a pleasing sight at times of high winds and heavy thunder storms, to observe the numerous squadrons of these Spanish curlews [White Ibises] driving to and fro, turning and tacking about, high up in the air, when by their various evolutions in the different and opposite currents of the wind high in the clouds, their silvery white plumage gleams and sparkles like the brightest crystal, reflecting the sun-beams that dart upon them between the dark clouds.

When not feeding, White Ibises often roost in trees. This species is found from the southeastern United States and northwest Mexico to Peru and Venezuela; it also occurs in the Greater Antilles. Okefenokee Swamp, Georgia.

As I continue my observations, the birds alight on the flats and immediately begin to probe the mud as they walk, each changing direction continuously. Their snow-white plumage and fiery red bill and legs, as well as their white eyes, which appear pale blue in the field, make identification of this bird unmistakable. However, not all the individuals of this flock are pure white. With light undersides, brown wings, and a brownish, soiled appearance on the head and neck, immature ibises forage alongside the adults.

I focus my telescope on one bird and observe its movements as it searches with its sense of touch. It repeatedly thrusts its entire bill into the mud, coating its proboscis and face with the dark substrate. Suddenly, the ibis jerks up its head with a struggling fiddler crab caught between its mandibles. With a few quick movements, the ibis works the crab up to its mouth, and in an instant it is swallowed. As in all North American ibises, the White Ibis does not often pursue its prey; the initial contact with a prey item is the moment of either capture or miss. Also, as observed in a number of heron species, the juvenile birds are less efficient than the adults at securing a meal.

The White Ibis has a varied diet including crayfish from inland freshwater habitats, fiddler crabs from coastal brackish water areas, aquatic insects, fish, and other small vertebrates such as snakes. A curious method used to capture crayfish has been reported for this bird. The ibis is presumably able to detect a crayfish burrow—and therefore a crayfish—by the small mound of excavated mud at the hole's entrance. After detection, the bird pushes part of the mound back into the burrow and waits. Then, when the crayfish appears at the tunnel's entrance to eject the mud, the ibis reaches quickly with its fifteen-centimeter-long bill to grasp the crustacean.

As with Snowy Egrets, White Ibises also are a core species in feeding aggregations in that other species of waders are attracted to areas in which the gregarious ibises are foraging. The attraction of other species, however, is not without a price: ibises are often robbed of their catch by such birds as the Great Egret. In an ibis population studied by ecologist James Kushlan, 90 percent of prey larger than ten centimeters was stolen as ibises handled their catch. In fact, some birds would drop a large prey item rather than risk its loss during manipulation and positioning for swallowing.

Observers of White Ibis flocks in southern Florida may have occasion to doubt their senses when an apparently pink bird appears amidst a snow-white assemblage, but they don't need to wipe their binocular lenses! In the early 1960s eggs of South American Scarlet Ibises were transplanted to White Ibis nests in Florida in an attempt to introduce the crimson bird to northern shores. Some of these eggs hatched, the chicks matured, and subsequently a few brilliantly colored birds hybridized with native White Ibises. As a result, today there is a handful of pink descendants gliding across Florida skies. In January 1990, I was fortunate to see one of these rare birds in Everglades National Park. Its salmon-pink body and paler head and neck were a visual treat among the background of white birds. Although I admittedly enjoyed the view, as an ecologist I realize it is highly ill-advised to introduce exotic species into natural biological communities. Furthermore, if it is the pink color that is so tantalizing, the Florida and Gulf coasts boast their own coral-colored bird: the Roseate Spoonbill.

The spoonbill is a close relative of the ibises and is often found in association with White Ibises on feeding grounds or at roosts along the Gulf coast. In flight the spoonbill belies its relationship to the ibises by holding its neck and legs outstretched and by flying in a diagonal formation. Its pale pink plumage is highlighted with crimson patches on its wings and chest and has given rise to its colloquial name, flame bird. Its legs are pink, its spatulate bill is greenish gray, its eyes are red, and the bare skin of its head is pale green with a black band running around the base of the head.

The Roseate Spoonbill feeds on fish, aquatic insects, and tiny crustaceans in freshwater ponds and sloughs and in saline coastal waters by sweeping its sensitive, flattened bill from side to side.

The Roseate Spoonbill (*Ajaia ajaja*) is a large (approximately eighty-centimeter) wader with brilliant pink, white, and orange plumage; a long, green, spatulate bill; and a red iris and legs. Ding Darling National Wildlife Refuge, Florida.

Occasionally it submerges its head in pursuit of a meal. As it arcs its bill through the water, it snaps up anything it comes in contact with. Thus, like ibises, the spoonbill hunts by touch. Whereas minute crustaceans are swallowed instantly, small fish are often beaten on the water's surface before swallowing. Feeding time is usually from dusk to dawn, although I have observed Roseate Spoonbills foraging in broad daylight in southern Florida. When hunting, as a spoonbill swings its bill back and forth, it will interrupt these movements to raise its head

to scan for danger. At times, spoonbills may move excitedly through the water to herd schools of minnows.

Due to their specialized feeding apparatus and diet, Roseate Spoonbills require warm, shallow water with little or no tidal range. Being gregarious waders, spoonbills actively forage alongside each other as well as in the vicinity of several species of egrets and herons. Moreover, Roseate Spoonbills may almost rub shoulders with a related bird that also hunts with an acute sense of touch: the Wood Stork.

The Roseate Spoonbill feeds by swinging its bill from side to side, feeling for prey, as it shuffles through shallow water.

Roseate Spoonbills perform various displays at their nests to both repel interlopers and attract mates.

By foraging at different depths, searching for different prey, and using different feeding techniques, wading birds effectively partition the resource base, thereby limiting competition and permitting coexistence. And if the food resource, such as fish, is superabundant, then there is plenty for all and many species can feed side by side. Ding Darling National Wildlife Refuge, Florida.

OPPOSITE TOP:
Immature Roseate Spoonbills are paler than adults. Merritt Island National Wildlife Refuge, Florida.

OPPOSITE BOTTOM:
Like many other long-legged wading birds, Roseate Spoonbills nest in colonies. This species ranges from southern Florida through Mexico to northern Argentina and is also found in the Greater Antilles.

North America's only native stork, this bird stands over one meter tall, has white plumage with black flight and tail feathers, and lacks feathers on its charcoal crown—hence its local name, flinthead. It often can be seen perched in a hunched posture on a snag, its black legs contrasting markedly with its pink feet. Although it may appear somewhat ungainly on the ground, the Wood Stork is graceful in the air, with its impressive wingspan and extended neck. I have observed storks soaring on rising thermals, spiraling to altitudes at which they appeared as mere specks against a blue sky.

The Wood Stork's long, stout, decurved bill is equipped with many nerve endings for detecting potential prey, the bulk of which is fish but also includes crayfish, amphibians, mollusks, and insects. In addition, baby alligators, turtles, avian nestlings, and crabs are taken. As the Wood Stork shuffles through shallow water, it swings its half-submerged, partially opened bill from side to side. When a fish above a certain size is encountered, the contact triggers a rapid bill-snap, one of the quickest reflex actions among vertebrates.

This highly colonial bird, also known as the Wood Ibis, hunts in coastal mangrove swamps and inland freshwater marshes and cypress swamps in the southeastern United States and along the Gulf coast. Crucial to the survival of this species are seasonally drying aquatic habitats. As a pond, for example, begins to evaporate during the south-

In flight, Roseate Spoonbills extend their necks and sometimes spiral upward on thermals, rising to great heights. Aransas Bay, Texas.

OVERLEAF PAGES:
The Roseate Spoonbill experienced a severe decline in the United States from the mid-1800s to the early 1900s due to habitat loss. Plume hunting, too, took its toll, as did disturbance of nesting colonies. Today, only a relict population remains, which is gradually increasing thanks to strict protective measures. Ding Darling National Wildlife Refuge, Florida.

The Wood Stork (*Mycteria americana*) is a large (ninety-five- to one-hundred-five-centimeter), ibis-like stork with a white body, black flight feathers, a stout, black, downcurved bill, black iris and legs, and dark feet, which are sometimes pink.

The bayous and swamps of Atchafalaya Basin, Louisiana, are declining due to the dredging of channels, creation of levees, and subsequent drainage.

The Wood Stork hunts in swamps and marshes for its favorite prey—fish, crayfish, amphibians, and other small items. It is a highly gregarious species found from the southern United States to northern Argentina.

The southern blue flag is an iris found in freshwater swamps and marshes along the Atlantic coast of North America.

ern Florida dry season, it contracts, thereby concentrating the fish. Such prey concentrations are critical to the storks to gather enough food to raise their young. Unfortunately, the massive development of wetlands in southern Florida and the diversion of fresh water to urban and agricultural areas have had a major detrimental impact on the Wood Stork population. As a result, this singular bird, which gropes for its dinner, is listed as an endangered species in the United States.

The Wood Stork is not alone among aquatic birds with its ominous designation. Half a continent away the most celebrated endan-

gered North American bird is en route to its breeding grounds in the Canadian Northwest Territories. The Whooping Crane, North America's tallest denizen of the wetlands, has teetered on the brink of extinction. Interestingly, like the Wood Stork, the Whooper has white plumage with jet-black flight feathers. However, the similarity ends there. Unlike the somewhat grotesque stork, the Whooper is a stately bird with golden eyes, black legs, red facial skin, a crimson crown, and a large "bustle."

The Whoopers that migrate to Wood Buffalo National Park in Canada comprise a relict population that winters in the shallow saltwater bays of Aransas National Wildlife Refuge off the Texas coast. Farther west an introduced population of Whooping Cranes makes its springtime journey from Bosque del Apache National Wildlife Refuge in New Mexico to its breeding grounds in Grays Lake National Wildlife Refuge in Idaho. The wetlands of Bosque del Apache are critical to the winter survival of these Whoopers as well as other aquatic birds. Encompassing the bottomlands of the Rio Grande, Bosque del Apache represents yet another kind of wetland found in North America: the riparian, or riverine, wetland.

Riparian wetlands typically occur as green margins along rivers and streams. Seasonal or periodic flooding saturates these areas with generous supplies of fresh water and thereby determines the hydrologic

By extending its wings while hunting, the Wood Stork may startle prey into motion or attract prey to the shade. The Wood Stork's bill is equipped with a generous supply of nerve endings, thus affording it a great sensitivity to touch.

OPPOSITE TOP:
Due to loss of habitat and the control of water flow in southern Florida, the Wood Stork population has declined markedly; consequently, this sole North American stork is now endangered.

OPPOSITE BOTTOM:
The Wood Stork feeds by swinging its half-submerged bill from side to side. If a prey item of suitable size is felt, a bill-snap reflex is triggered.

The Whooping Crane *(Grus americana)* is
North America's tallest bird (approximately
one hundred thirty centimeters) and has a
white body, red crown and facial skin, gold-
en eyes, slate legs, and large "bustle." Due
mainly to loss of habitat, the Whooper has
declined dramatically and is critically
endangered.

Immature Whooping Cranes have
brown feathers scattered throughout
their white plumage; their necks are
tawny. They remain under the care of
their parents for almost one year and
will themselves be able to breed in five
years. Aransas National Wildlife
Refuge, Texas.

Freshwater ponds, such as this one in Yosemite National Park, California, are found throughout North America and support an abundance of wildlife.

Riparian wetlands, like the Merced River in California, are dynamic ecosystems that experience dramatic seasonal changes, such as flooding. Because they link together both aquatic and upland habitats, riparian wetlands are rich in wildlife.

conditions that support an abundance of life-forms. As a transition zone, or ecotone, between aquatic and upland terrestrial ecosystems, a riparian habitat is usually richer in species than adjacent areas. Deer, beavers, muskrats, otters, waterfowl, wading birds, songbirds, snakes, frogs, fish, and many invertebrates populate these productive wetlands.

Riparian wetlands are exceptionally dynamic ecosystems that exist in a ceaseless state of flux. The rhythm of the changing seasons is mirrored in the alternating flooding and retreating of water and in the concomitant processes of erosion and deposition. At one time building

up its floodplain, at another time reclaiming it, the pulse of the river leaves its ever-changing signature on the face of the land.

Detritus originating from the foliage of streamside trees and other vegetation forms the base of the food chain in most streams. Legions of aquatic decomposers are at hand to reduce the fallen leaves to ever-smaller particles, thereby releasing stored-up nutrients. As streams erode their beds and banks, minerals are released for uptake by plants. Climate, water volume, topography, soil type, and quality of vegetation all have their roles to play in the seasonal drama of these places. The

Whooping Cranes feed in open areas and constantly scan for danger. Their diet consists of insects, small vertebrates, roots, and grains, which they procure by taking long strides and pecking at the ground.

The Whooping Crane's black wingtips are apparent when the bird is in flight. From a population low of under twenty birds at the turn of the twentieth century, Whoopers now number slightly over two hundred, both wild and captive, thanks to concerted efforts of various conservation agencies.

OVERLEAF PAGES:
The Whooping Crane migrates between its breeding range in Wood Buffalo National Park in Canada and its wintering grounds in Aransas National Wildlife Refuge on the Texas Gulf coast. A small introduced population winters in Bosque del Apache National Wildlife Refuge, New Mexico, and spends the remainder of the year in Grays Lake National Wildlife Refuge in Idaho. Discussions are currently under way to decide whether a second introduced population, which would be nonmigratory, should be established in Florida. Because adults typically associate only with their mates and young, it is unusual to see more than two adults together. These four may be five-year-old birds just prior to pairing.

The Platte River forms one of the continent's most extensive riparian wetlands. The dynamic flux of water shapes and reshapes the river banks and associated islands.

particular constellation of these factors in a given area bestows uniqueness to each riparian wetland.

Major distinctions, however, are recognizable between riverine environments in the eastern United States and in the West. Bottomland hardwood forests in the East, especially in the southeastern United States, occur in broad alluvial valleys exemplified in the lower Mississippi River valley. Many tree species take root in these fertile regions. Similarly, farther north, maple swamps may cover large expanses of lowlands. In contrast, riparian wetlands in the arid West usually form narrow fringes of cottonwoods and willows along waterways. These linear verdant oases often stand in stark contrast to the surrounding parched desert. Bosque del Apache is a typical western riparian wetland, save for its managed irrigation system and its most celebrated avian winter visitor, the Whooping Crane.

The Whooper's diet includes insects, crayfish, frogs, small mammals, fish, roots, tubers, berries, and grain. This diversified menu varies depending on whether the crane is on its breeding or wintering grounds or en route between the two. For example, Whoopers wintering in the Gulf of Mexico eat crayfish, blue crabs, and clams—items unavailable in other parts of their range.

As it forages, a Whooper takes long strides, lowers its head to peer, and then pecks at a food item. Whooping Cranes are extremely wary and therefore feed in open areas where they can survey large expanses for danger. The wilderness freshwater marshlands of Wood Buffalo National Park in Canada afford such an opportunity and support the last unassisted, wild breeding population of Whoopers. Likewise, Aransas National Wildlife Refuge on the Texas Gulf coast provides saltwater habitat for the wintering wild population, while the riparian wetlands of Bosque del Apache offer winter habitat for the introduced population. During migration cranes land to feed in midwestern grainfields where historically they were especially vulnerable to hunters.

The Sandhill Crane, a smaller relative of the Whooper, has diet and feeding behaviors similar to those of its cousin. Ranging throughout North America and south into Cuba, the Sandhill occurs in at least five recognized subspecies, including the Lesser, Greater, and Canadian races. The oldest fossils of any living bird are those of this gray-plumaged crane with golden brown eyes, black legs, and a red crown. Individual birds may have a rusty tinge to their plumage, which is produced by painting themselves with mud rich in iron oxides. And, like the Whooper, Sandhills are considered to be one of North America's most beautiful birds. In A Sand County Almanac (1949), Aldo Leopold had these words to say about cranes:

> Our ability to perceive quality in nature begins, as in
> art, with the pretty. It expands through successive stages
> of the beautiful to values as yet uncaptured by language.
> The quality of cranes lies, I think, in this higher gamut,
> as yet beyond the reach of words.

Sandhills prefer freshwater wetlands such as marshes, wooded swamps, bogs, and flooded fields, as well as prairies and cultivated areas. Feeding takes place mainly on land. In Bosque del Apache, Sandhills are often seen foraging side by side with Whoopers. Their diet consists of insects, spiders, snails, roots, tubers, berries, grain, and

herbage. Gravel is consumed to help grind up seeds in the gizzard. Sandhills also take small mammals and occasionally young birds. One Canadian study showed that Sandhills eat Snow Goose eggs and Willow Ptarmigan chicks. In high arctic grassy wetlands, cranes were observed feeding on arctic willow tubers by snipping off the flower spikes and then jabbing at the ground around the tubers to extract them. Lemmings are also a diet item in the Arctic. Sandhills hunt these small rodents by peering into their burrows and then, if a lemming is discovered, thrusting their bill into the chamber to grasp the furry morsel.

Large birds that they are, cranes must have running starts against the wind to get airborne. Once aloft, they can fly at altitudes of eight hundred meters. Unlike herons, which tuck in their necks, cranes fly with outstretched necks, constantly uttering vocalizations from the heights as if to announce their passage, presumably so flock members can keep in contact with each other.

Cranes belong to a worldwide family (Gruidae) that includes fifteen species that share many morphological and behavioral features. The ibis and spoonbill family (Threskiornithidae) consists of about thirty

OPPOSITE:
The Sandhill Crane (*Grus canadensis*) is a tall (one-hundred- to one-hundred-ten-centimeter) bird with rust-stained gray plumage, a red crown, gold iris, and slate-colored bill and legs. (Photograph by William Weber.)

During both spring and fall migrations, Sandhill Cranes converge on the Platte River in great abundance.

species and, besides the obvious bill-shape difference between ibises and spoonbills, the group is rather homogeneous. The heron family (Ardeidae), on the other hand, includes about sixty species that exhibit a greater degree of morphological and behavioral diversity than the cranes or ibises. For example, it is hard to believe that Least Bitterns and Great Egrets are closely related; yet, they are. Overall, in each of these avian families, nature demonstrates wonderful variations on a theme. There is one noteworthy family, however, that exhibits no variations simply because it includes only one member! Standing alone among wetland birds, the Limpkin, due to its unique morphology, is classified by taxonomists as the sole member of its family (Aramidae).

The oddness of the Limpkin results not just from its name—which refers to its halting gait—but to its curious position as a link between cranes and rails. While it shares skeletal and feathering characteristics with cranes, the Limpkin's behavior, digestive system, and nesting traits are akin to those of rails. For example, when alarmed, the Limpkin can retreat quickly through dense vegetation, much as do rails. Similarly, the Limpkin often ends its flight by abruptly dropping into protective vegetation in a raillike manner. Another unusual feature of this wetland inhabitant is its wailing call, which has inspired such names as mourning widow and crying bird.

The Limpkin, which resembles a large-bodied ibis, dwells in

In the spring, shoreline marsh grasses provide a buffer against erosion. Chincoteague National Wildlife Refuge, Virginia.

freshwater marshes and swamps, and in mangrove wetlands, from extreme southern Georgia through Florida. This brown-plumaged, lightly streaked bird, with brown eyes and brownish black legs, feeds on mollusks—especially snails and mussels—small aquatic vertebrates, worms, and insects. It is particularly fond of the apple snail *(Pomacea)*, also a favorite of the Everglades Kite, and, like the kite, its distribution is more or less limited to where this snail occurs. To secure this diet, the largely nocturnal Limpkin applies various foraging behaviors. It can hunt visually on land and in clear water, and tactilely by probing ibis fashion among surface vegetation and in turbid water.

After a freshwater mussel is taken, the Limpkin is faced with the problem of extracting the creature from its shell. To perform the extraction, the Limpkin typically transports a mussel to an exposed surface, positions the mollusk with the ventral edges of the valves pointing upward, and then hammers the armor repeatedly with its powerful bill. When enough damage has been inflicted, the bird works its slender lower mandible between the valves to sever the adductor muscles. Next, the soft creature is removed, positioned higher in the bill, and subsequently swallowed. Because a Limpkin may repeatedly use the same site for extractions, a considerable pile of discarded mussel shells may accumulate.

Limpkins employ similar methods in removing snails from their protective spires. After the mollusk is transported to an exposed area, the Limpkin delivers blows to the operculum—the shell's door—until it is damaged enough that the bird can slide its lower mandible into the shell to snip the muscle that attaches the creature to its spiral home. Interestingly, the Limpkin's lower mandible curves to the right

The Limpkin feeds primarily on apple snails and freshwater mussels by hunting visually or by probing in ibis fashion.

The Limpkin (*Aramus guarauna*) is a medium-bodied (approximately seventy-centimeter), ibislike bird with light streaks in its brown plumage; a long, dark, downcurved bill; a brown iris; and greenish brown legs.

Although Limpkins most often roost in reed thickets, trees are sometimes used. This species is found in the southeastern United States, Mexico, parts of South America, and the West Indies. Loxahatchee National Wildlife Refuge, Florida.

to accommodate the curvature of the shell. Once the muscle attachment is severed, the snail is removed and gobbled down. Afterwards, the Limpkin continues its solitary hunt for further delicacies.

Due to its selective diet of snails and mussels, the Limpkin encounters little competition among other wading birds for food. Similarly, the Cattle Egret, because it prefers hunting in terrestrial habitats, only minimally interferes with other foraging waders. In a sense, the egret, like the Limpkin, is a specialist that enjoys a food resource largely ignored by other wetland birds. Thus, Cattle Egrets experience little competition for food. The situation of the Cattle Egret, however, begs the question of whether birds that do forage in the same habitat compete with one another for sustenance. For example, at first glance numerous species of waders feeding in a brackish pond may appear to be exploiting the same resource. After all, they are

concentrated in the same body of water. However, closer scrutiny reveals that each species is in fact selectively focused on only a limited portion of the resource. Differences in heron sizes, for instance, sort them according to what depth a given species can stalk in. While Green-backed Herons are restricted to hunting in extreme shallows or from nearshore tangles of vegetation, Great Blues can wade to substantial depths. Furthermore, Great Blues can tackle sizable fish that would be impossible to handle for a Green-back, or even for midsized herons. Different species of wading birds also feed on qualitatively different kinds of prey. While Great Blues, Green-backs, and Snowy Egrets pursue fish, White Ibises scour the shoreline for fiddler crabs, Roseate Spoonbills sift through the water in search of minute aquatic invertebrates, and Least Bitterns snap at dragonflies among dense reeds.

In addition, activity rhythms differ and thereby reduce interfer-

In flight, Limpkins resemble ibises by flying with their necks outstretched. During short flights their toes and legs dangle; on longer flights they hold their legs straight out behind, as do herons.

Ponds, like this one at Chincoteague National Wildlife Refuge, Virginia, exist year-round, although their levels change seasonally.

Sawgrass prairies in Everglades National Park depend on the slow but steady flow of fresh water from Lake Okeechobee. Although eighty kilometers wide, the Shark River, which floods the Everglades, is only fifteen centimeters deep.

ence among waders. As the sun sets on the western horizon, the diurnal herons and ibises retreat to their roosts, while night-herons and Limpkins commence feeding.

Overall, the resources of a given wetland tend to be partitioned among the various species that dwell within it, thus permitting numerous species to coexist. There is, however, some overlap of resource use among birds in a wetland habitat. But if the resource, such as fish, is in good supply, competition is minimal and coexistence becomes possible.

Wetlands, especially coastal estuaries, often teem with life, which is sustained by the bountiful production of these ecosystems. In fact, as we have seen, estuaries are some of the most productive ecosystems on the planet. The energy transfers of sunlight to phytoplankton to herbivorous zooplankton to carnivorous zooplankton to fish, for example, form the energetic backbone of the ecosystem, which provides for a rich resource base. Consequently, wetlands are havens for wildlife, with wading birds as the ultimate expression of the pulse of life in these places.

It is early evening in the salt marsh, and the setting sun vanishes behind a stand of marsh grass. The tide pools and mudflats that earlier were conspicuous elements of the landscape have disappeared, temporarily obliterated by the swelling tide. Insects dance in the air above the *Spartina* meadow while a Clapper Rail clucks quietly from its hidden refuge. Several Snowy Egrets and a Glossy Ibis are perched on snags along the shore. The ibis turns its head over its shoulder and, with its sicklelike bill, preens its back feathers. Similarly, an egret stretches its neck upright and works its bill down along its throat feathers, primping its white shawl. For now there is time to loaf and groom. But soon, as the season progresses, the business of courtship, breeding, and parenthood will monopolize the time and energy of these and other wading birds across the North American wetlands.

Barrier island sounds, like Roanoke Bay in North Carolina, are often estuaries and habitat for clams, crabs, fish, and long-legged wading birds.

2. Courtship,
Breeding, and
Parenthood

PRECEDING PAGES:
Many wading birds, such as these
Great Egrets, are colonial nesters
and require the stimulation of nest-
ing neighbors in order to breed.
Aransas National Wildlife Refuge,
Texas.

166

As the midday sun rises successively higher in the sky, and a lingering winter chill gives way to vernal warmth, wetlands across North America become the stage on which wading birds perform the drama of procreation. From saltwater marshes to freshwater ponds to coastal keys, herons, ibises, storks, and cranes are faced with the challenge of securing breeding territories, attracting mates, and coupling, with the eventual outcome of a raucous brood to care for. The behaviors associated with these activities are some of the most spectacular observed in wading birds, although they are some of the least-witnessed behaviors in this group. In reproductive behavior, as in feeding behavior, one can observe similarities, with variations on a theme, among closely related wading birds.

Members of the heron family show a remarkable degree of similarity in the various displays exhibited in the breeding season. At this time morphological and behavioral changes occur. In Great Blue Herons the plumes on the back of the head and nape lengthen, the iris color intensifies to red, the lores turn light green, sometimes brilliant blue, and the legs adopt an orange glow. The Great Egret, too, develops a spectacular breeding plumage with over three dozen lengthy aigrettes that extend beyond the tail feathers, bright green lores, and an orange bill. In the Cattle Egret the crown, nape, lower neck, and back turn a striking orange-buff color, while the bare areas, including the bill and legs, flush a bright scarlet. Night-herons also sport their finery, which includes several long, thin plumes that stream from the crown.

Typically, males lay claim to breeding territories and nest sites at the onset of the season. The chosen site is defended against rivals first by threat displays and, if those are unconvincing, by actual pursuits and wing-to-wing combat. A characteristic threat display consists of raised crest feathers and a forward neck stretch accompanied by erected plumes and a harsh cry. In Least Bitterns the threat display consists of leaning forward with neck retracted and wings spread. Male Green-backed Herons can be quite pugnacious toward intruders in that they readily perform pursuit flights, often accompanied by a raspy "raah-raah" call. During such presentations the red mouth-lining is exposed, which may serve as a further signal for intimidation.

As the breeding season progresses, males increasingly tend to their mates, spending less time being hostile toward would-be interlopers and more time in courtship displays. Consequently, the nest territory contracts in size until it includes just the nest and a small area sur-

In the breeding season, rookeries come alive with activity. Herons, egrets, and ibises don their nuptial finery, clamor for nest sites, thwart intruders, and advertise for mates. This is a Great Egret in courtship display.

rounding it. With the gradual increase of relinquished areas, late-arriving males have a better opportunity to establish their own territories.

The territorial displays of males serve both as a threat to rivals and as an advertisement to females. Initially, however, even females are repulsed, but soon their presence is tolerated. Reddish Egret males ceremoniously court females by tossing back their heads to flaunt their shaggy neck feathers. (Females, too, may perform this behavior.) To further impress a prospective mate, a male may walk circles around her, tossing back his head and extending his wings. Black-crowned Night-Herons advertise the possession of a nest site to females by swaying from side to side and then arching the back and lowering the head, accompanied by a hissing sound. If a female is interested, she will perform a ritualized ceremony by erecting her crown and neck feathers. The male then follows suit and the pair-bond is initiated. This is later strengthened by mutual feather nibbling and bill contact. Male Least Bitterns announce their readiness for a mate by emitting a dovelike cooing call, which, according to noted ornithologist Frank Chapman, "floats over the marsh like the voice of a spirit bird."

The stretch display—in which the male extends his neck, points his bill skyward, flexes his legs, and then sways his head from side to side as he lowers it—is a behavioral repertoire characteristic of most male herons trying to tempt females to the nest site. In Yellow-crowned Night-Herons this behavior consists of a slow, steady neck extension with the bill held horizontally, followed by a rapid retraction of the neck toward the scapular region. Erected scapular plumes, a lowered breast, bulging eyes, and flexed legs accompany the neck retraction, which concludes with an upward pointing bill and a subdued "whoop" call. An erect posture follows.

Other behavioral enticements, as observed in the Great Blue Heron for example, include circle flights, fluffing neck feathers, and audibly snapping the mandibles closed. A typical display of Tricolored Herons consists of stretching the neck and bobbing the head alternately from left to right; this performance is accompanied by bill snapping. The Tricolored's melding of the stretch and snap displays into a single performance is unique among herons. In addition, the males of this colorful species can be so absorbed with territory defense that they shun feeding until the pair-bond is formed. In the Tricolored, as in most members of this family, once the pair-bond is initiated, partners may engage in mutual preening and mutual bill clappering in which they gently grasp the other's bill and vibrate their mandibles around it. Soft vocalizations may be exchanged at these times.

It is characteristically the male's chore to gather and present sticks to the female for placement (although these roles are reversed in the Least Bittern). When he returns with nest material, it is offered ceremoniously with raised crown and scapular and neck plumes. The female responds similarly as she receives the stick. Then, the male may

OPPOSITE:
Many species of long-legged waders build crude nests, which are little more than platforms of sticks. Nest locations can range from the ground to treetops. These are Roseate Spoonbills at Ding Darling National Wildlife Refuge, Florida.

169

The iris, bill, and legs of the Cattle Egret turn bright red in the breeding season. In addition, buff highlights appear on the otherwise white plumage. Peapatch Island, Delaware.

nibble his mate's feathers as she works the stick into the nest. During nest construction, one mate is always present at the nest to thwart would-be twig thieves.

Whereas in most herons sticks are passed between mates from bill to bill during nest construction, the stick-passing ceremony is poorly developed in Great Egrets. In this species the male simply drops the stick into the nest; the female then grasps it and works it into the structure. And in American Bitterns it is apparently the female that builds the nest single-handedly without the assistance of her mate. In contrast, Reddish Egrets are unique in that both partners gather nest material. An egret returning to the nest may engage in an elaborate twig-passing ritual in which a stretch display is performed; the mate responds likewise, and both partake in head tossing and bill snapping.

It is not uncommon for some heron species to recycle their nests. Male Black-crowned Night-Herons and Great Blues typically reclaim nest sites that were used by them in previous years. Similarly, Green-backed Herons often reuse their previous year's nests or perhaps build on an old night-heron nest.

Nests are usually crude platforms of sticks lined with finer material. There is much variation in the placement of nests among, and even

within, species. The Great Blue Heron's nest, which is a shallow struc-ture of sticks slightly greater than one meter in diameter, is typically situated in the crown of a tall tree—a cottonwood, for example. However, Great Blue nests have also been observed on the ground and in low vegetation. In a mixed-species colony, Great Blue nests are usu-ally placed higher than those of other species. In Tricolored Herons, the nest is typically located in vegetation within three meters of the ground or situated on the ground in reeds. Rookeries may contain thousands of mated pairs and may be composed almost exclusively of Tricoloreds, or they may be a mixed-species colony. In a mixed colony Tricoloreds may locate their nest anywhere within the rookery from the periphery to the heart of the aggregation. Cattle Egrets, too, often nest in mixed colonies of Little Blue Herons, Snowy Egrets, and Black-crowned Night-Herons. In fact, the egrets may require the presence of other breeding birds to stimulate their own reproductive behaviors.

Besides the social stimulation of breeding behavior in some species, colonial nesting may have other advantages. Some ornitholo-gists maintain that coloniality may provide increased vigilance—that is, more eyes to detect a predator. Some reported predators of adult wading birds include Ospreys, Red-tailed Hawks, and Peregrine

Immature Yellow-crowned Night-Herons take time to develop their hunting skills. Chincoteague National Wildlife Refuge, Virginia.

The Chesapeake Bay, formed by the overflow of the Susquehanna River, is an estuary that serves as spawning grounds for a multitude of marine organisms.

This American alligator has just captured a Common Moorhen in Loxahatchee National Wildlife Refuge, Florida.

Falcons, and I have circumstantial evidence that a Great Horned Owl killed two Yellow-crowned Night-Herons. Birds may also be attracted to a nesting site that lies outside the territories of predators. Bald Eagles, for example, are known to take Great Blue Heron nestlings, so it would be to the herons' advantage to nest together in an area that falls outside an eagle's haunt. Another benefit of colonial nesting may be increased opportunities for finding food. It has been postulated that colony members may be able to determine which of their neighbors are successful at procuring food by observing birds returning to the colony. If a neighbor returns laden with food for its young, then it would be beneficial to follow that individual when it departs the nest for further hunting. If a neighbor returns empty-handed, then one should not fly off in the direction from which the unsuccessful bird arrived. Although plausible, this information-sharing hypothesis continues to be debated by ornithologists.

Not all wading birds enjoy the company of neighbors. Least Bitterns are mostly solitary nesters but occasionally are loosely colonial, probably to exploit superabundant food resources. The bittern's nest is a flimsy platform composed of grass stalks and reeds, both living and dried. It is usually situated in emergent vegetation, such as reeds, just above the water's surface. Nests may also be placed in bushes, and in those locations the structure may be made of twigs. American Bitterns are also solitary nesters. As with their smaller cousins, the nest is constructed in emergent vegetation, typically reeds. Although it is well concealed, a careful observer may be able to detect a path of trampled vegetation that leads to it.

In most herons, ritualized courtship displays and copulation occur on or near the nest. Three to five pale bluish green eggs are incubated by both parents for about twenty-one to twenty-five days. A ritualized greeting ceremony is often performed between mates during nest relief. In the event the clutch is destroyed by crows, raccoons, or snakes, many herons, like the Green-back, can produce a replacement clutch. It has been reported that incubating Least Bitterns show little fear of humans. In fact, some birds permit themselves to be picked up, and Audubon claimed that, in the afternoon, sleeping bitterns can be caught by hand.

Because the eggs are laid on alternate days and incubation begins with the first, hatching is asynchronous—that is, staggered. Consequently, the chicks are of different sizes, and the youngest, which is also the weakest, often succumbs to battering by its siblings and ultimate starvation. Although in years of plenty such brood reduction is minimized, studies have shown that, regardless of food availability, the last-hatched chick of a brood of three has a growth rate significantly lower than that of its siblings.

When it emerges from the shell, a heron chick sports sparse, pale down feathers. Except for this scroungy down, the gangly bird's body could be overlooked, because in appearance the diminutive frame seems little more than an excuse to connect a weighty bill with lanky legs and feet.

With the exception of the American Bittern, care is provided by both parents. In Snowy Egrets, when the chicks are only a few days old, they seize the parents' bill crosswise to elicit feeding. In about twenty to twenty-five days after hatching, the juvenile egrets are ready to leave the nest and face the outside world. Life, however, is not auspicious for newly fledged Snowys. Banding studies have shown that mortality

Most species of herons lay three to five pale, greenish blue eggs. The eggs are laid on alternate days and incubation begins with the first. This is a Cattle Egret nest on Peapatch Island, Delaware.

Incubation is by both parents in most species of wading birds. Moreover, both parents take turns in feeding the young, which are covered with down feathers. These young Cattle Egrets have an ungainly appearance typical of members of the heron family.

among egrets during their first year of life is roughly 70 percent. Similarly, the most precarious period in a Great Blue's life is during its first year, especially during the first five months after hatching. Many fatal accidents occur when chicks begin clambering from the nest and inadvertently end up on the ground where predators lurk. Some predators, like raccoons, may raid the nest itself. In the face of these and other dangers, only about 30 percent of the nestlings will survive their first year.

In Yellow-crowned Night-Herons, the young are ready to leave the nest after about twenty-five days, at which time they accompany

In about twenty to twenty-five days after hatching, most nestlings, like this Cattle Egret, are ready to venture from the nest.

These immature Little Blue Herons will be fed by their parents up to, and even a little beyond, fledging.

In the Everglades, sawgrass is a dominant plant of freshwater marshes. When the prickly blades die, they fall to the marsh floor and there decompose and accumulate as peat. The peat, in turn, serves as a natural fertilizer for marshland trees and other plants.

their parents to the feeding grounds where they learn the art of hunting. At first, their attempts to capture prey are rather awkward, but soon enough the herons perfect their hunting skills. Yellow-crowns, like most herons, become reproductively mature at two years old. The Cattle Egret, however, is exceptional in that this relatively precocious species is able to breed in its first year.

Just as herons sport their springtime nuptial finery, ibises display their courtship dress. While Glossy and White-faced Ibises develop a metallic sheen and intensify their facial colors, White Ibises transform into particolored extravaganzas. Their facial skin, bill, legs, and feet become brilliant scarlet, and a red sac develops from the chin. During moments of emotional excitement, the chin pouch distends.

Breeding habitat varies both within and among ibis species. Glossys nest in many kinds of trees and shrubs that overhang water; both *Spartina* and *Phragmites* stands are also suitable. On the Atlantic coast these lustrous birds show a preference for nesting on dredge-spoil islands. Various species of herons and egrets, especially Black-crowned Night-Herons, often share a colony site with Glossy Ibises. The Glossy's sibling species, the White-faced Ibis, typically nests on the ground in low shrubs, cattails, or bulrushes, also in the company of herons and egrets.

Mangrove thickets along the Florida coast, willows, and other trees accommodate huge colonies of White Ibises. The neighborhood may also include egrets, Wood Storks, and Anhingas. In some parts of their range White Ibises may nest on matted-down clumps of needlerush. Such low-lying nests are vulnerable to exceptionally high tides; consequently about half of these nests are lost to inundating waters every breeding season.

As in herons, male ibises select and assiduously defend a breeding territory whose radius may be no longer than the distance to which a standing ibis can reach with the tip of his bill. Male White Ibises perform forward threat displays, which include horizontal posturing, neck extension, opened bill, and erected feathers. The red throat sac may also be inflated. Occasionally, if an intruder gets too close, the defender may pursue the interloper in flight.

To attract females, male White Ibises reach for branches with their decurved bills and nibble along the length of the limbs. These antics are interrupted intermittently with preening bouts to flaunt the male's plumage. Snap displays, much like those of herons, are also performed. Initially, inquisitive females are repulsed, but soon potential mates are accepted and may even be pursued for short distances.

Mutual feather nibbling helps to cement the pair-bond. The couple may also entwine their slender necks, which may be accompanied by low cooing sounds. Once the pair is established, nest construction commences. Males are the primary twig collectors, while females, after being presented with the materials, construct the nest, which is a circular platform with a cup-shaped depression. Copulation occurs at the nest site and is often followed by active preening. Occasionally, a

In about three weeks after hatching, Little Blue Herons are ready to try out their wings.

mated pair may usurp a neighbor's nest by evicting the resident, stabbing the eggs, and discarding the remnants.

In White Ibises, three to four pale bluish eggs, often with brown markings, are laid. In Glossy and White-faced Ibises, females incubate the greenish blue eggs throughout the night and part of the day; males perform their parental duty for a portion of the day. Mutual billing and preening, to the sound of soft cooing, often accompany nest relief.

Incubation begins only after the entire clutch is laid, although there are exceptions. Those eggs that have escaped the eyes of predators hatch in about three weeks. The hatchlings appear unibislike, with rather short bills. To receive a meal, the gawky chicks insert their bills into a parent's bill. At about three weeks old, the young, now looking like proper ibises, begin to venture from the nest. In another two weeks they are capable of flight and follow their parents to the feeding grounds where they continue to be fed for perhaps two weeks. Studies by ecologist Keith Bildstein in South Carolina have found that breeding success of White Ibis colonies is directly related to precipitation. In dry years, when crayfish become scarce, the number of fledged young declines markedly. Thus, the vagaries of weather play into the lives of these birds.

Courtship and reproduction in Roseate Spoonbills are similar to

Egret nestlings often compete vigorously for the attention of an adult laden with food. The youngest chick, which is the smallest, invariably loses in the scramble. Furthermore, the older siblings may harass and peck at their younger sibling. Thus, when food is scarce, the youngest chick usually perishes. Loxahatchee National Wildlife Refuge, Florida.

In two years this Little Blue Heron fledgling will molt its white plumage and attain the dark blue plumes of an adult. Peapatch Island, Delaware.

Eggs and nestlings of wading birds are vulnerable to various predators. Here, White-faced Ibis nests are eyed by Laughing Gulls, which wait for an unguarded moment to snatch an egg. West Bay, Galveston, Texas.

those activities in ibises. These salmon-colored birds often situate their rookeries on mangrove islets in estuaries. A male advertises a nesting territory by grasping nearby branches and shaking them vigorously. Often, a male will partially raise his wings to expose the brightly colored undersurfaces. With his back to the sun and the light shining through the openings between his wing feathers, the male enhances his appearance. Mutual bill clappering, stick presentations, hopping, and standing with bodies touching are behaviors that establish and maintain the pair-bond. Both birds defend the nest site from approaching

When heron and egret chicks are newly hatched, the adults typically drop food onto the nest floor or into the gaping mouths of the young. As they mature, the chicks become capable of grasping a parent's bill at the base to solicit gullet feeding.

colony members by performing threat displays, which include a neck extension with lowered head and raised wings.

The nest is a bulky structure of twigs lined with finer material such as leaves and grasses. Incubation begins with the first egg laid but is intermittent until the entire clutch of three to four eggs is present. A changing of the guard at the nest occurs two to three times daily and is preceded by a nest-relief call. Besides sharing incubation, both parents care for the young. The ungainly chicks beg by pumping their downy heads up and down while chattering; they then insert their bills into those of their parents to receive a meal. The young are left to their own devices in about six weeks. In a spoonbill colony on the Texas coast, nest success was roughly 50 percent—that is, half of the eggs produced young that eventually fledged. Survivorship is often reduced by Great-tailed Grackles taking eggs, by raccoons and bobcats preying on nestlings, or by starvation.

Wood Storks breed in large colonies with up to two dozen nests per tree, which can be situated in anything from clumps of mangroves to tall cypresses. By nesting in trees surrounded by water, storks may be inadvertently protecting their progeny—raccoons and other mammalian predators would have to risk the jaws of alligators in order to approach a stork colony. At the onset of the breeding season, male storks wander through the colony sparring with each other and performing ritualized preening behaviors to catch the eye of a female. If a female shows interest, the male typically nibbles her bill and, thus, seasonal matrimony is initiated. As in White Ibises, a Wood Stork pair may usurp the already completed nest of a neighboring pair by evicting the parents along with their eggs or chicks.

Parental responsibilities are shared between the mates. The three to four creamy white eggs are incubated for about one month in a stick-platform nest, often lined with Spanish moss. Sometimes the nests are so densely arranged that they touch. During nest relief, a simple but convincing ritualized ceremony is performed in which the incubating bird rises from the nest and greets its mate with open bill and subdued vocalizations. The arrival, in turn, often brings a token branch for placement in the nest structure.

During their first month of life, the chicks are incessantly attended, the indefatigable adults providing warmth, protection, and food. Meals are dropped onto the nest floor, which lends itself to a scramble by the rambunctious chicks. In just under two months the young are ready to take to the sky, albeit with some initial unsteadiness. Parental care, especially feeding, continues for another month until the fledglings can fend for themselves in their wetland home.

Although much is known about the breeding biology of wading birds, the reproductive behavior of the Limpkin remains somewhat of a mystery. These primarily nocturnal wetland dwellers breed in loose colonies in areas of favorable food supply. Nest construction, initiated by the male, is performed by both partners. The well-concealed nest is usually a bulky mass of reeds lined with finer material and is situated in tall marsh grass near water. The reeds, which can be partially decomposed, are interwoven with the living grasses. In some environments the nest is formed simply by trampling a depression in vegetation. Sometimes the nest is placed low in a shrub or as high as fifteen meters in a tree.

An average of six buff-brown eggs with dark markings is incubated by both parents. Moreover, both adults care for the young, which, like rail hatchlings, are generously covered with a dense, long down. The chicks leave the nest the same day they hatch, and soon thereafter the young become good swimmers and quite adept at slipping through dense marsh grasses. It takes one year for the young to develop the full adult plumage. Courtship displays, incubation times, parental behavior, fledgling success, and other aspects of Limpkin breeding biology remain undescribed.

In contrast to the dearth of information on Limpkin reproductive behavior, we know much about the breeding biology of a group of birds with perhaps the most colorful, vocal, and elaborately choreographed avian mating rituals: the cranes. Both Sandhill and Whooping Cranes

In winter, when their food supply diminishes in northern latitudes, wading birds migrate to warmer regions where they can continue to sustain themselves. Blackwater National Wildlife Refuge, Maryland.

partake in spectacular courtship displays that are best described in the words of foremost crane biologist Robert Allen in regard to a pair of Whoopers:

Suddenly one bird (the male?) began bowing his head and flapping his wings. At the same time he leaped stiffly into the air, an amazing bounce on stiffened legs that carried him nearly three feet off the ground. In the air he threw his head back so that the bill pointed skyward, neck arched over his back. Throughout this leap the great wings were constantly flapping, their long black flight feathers in striking contrast to the dazzling white of the rest of the plumage. The second bird (the female?) was facing the first when he reached the ground after completing the initial bounce. She ran forward a few steps, pumping her head up and down and flapping her wings. Then both birds leaped into the air, wings flapping, necks doubled up over their backs, legs thrust downward stiffly. Again they leaped, bouncing as if on pogo sticks. On the ground they ran towards each other, bowing and spreading their huge wings. Then another leap! The climax was almost frantic, both birds leaping two and three times in succession. Quickly it was all over, after about four minutes, and an extended period of preening followed.

These impressive displays, which are already initiated on the wintering grounds, are often accompanied by grass tossing in which a bird tears out a beakful of turf and, in a continuous motion, flings the clump skyward. It is during territorial disputes—and at other times perhaps for pure joy—that Whoopers emit the sound for which they are named. The loud bugling, or trumpeting, which can carry for over a kilometer and a half, is produced by a one-and-a-half-meter-long windpipe that is coiled like a French horn.

Sandhills and Whoopers build bulky nests of heaped grasses, reeds, and other coarse vegetation in the midst of a freshwater marsh or flooded prairie. Experienced pairs apparently return to their nest sites of previous years. Both parents incubate usually two eggs and care for the young. Hatching, which is asynchronous, is an arduous task and may take twenty-four hours to complete. The precocial chicks follow their parents soon thereafter. The adults, always vigilant, call to the young if danger is sensed. In the Florida subspecies of Sandhill Crane, danger may take the form of a raccoon, bobcat, or alligator. Due to these and other hazards, usually only one chick survives to fledge, which occurs several months after hatching. In both species of North American crane, strong bonds exist between individuals, which are maintained by contact calls. Not only do adults pair for life, the young remain with their parents for almost an entire year. The young themselves will be able to breed in five years.

As the season progresses and the sun climbs lower in the sky day after day, young cranes accompany their parents to ancestral wintering grounds. There are few spectacles that so poignantly signal the passage of time and the imminent approach of winter as the migration of cranes. However, cranes are not alone among wading birds in their autumnal peregrinations. In wetlands across North America, wading birds take wing, backlighted by brilliant orange sunsets, to begin their journeys to their southern winter homes.

3. The Rites of Passage

PRECEDING PAGES:
Formed when a portion of the
receding waters of the Gulf of
California was trapped, the Salton
Sea today provides habitat for
migrating and resident waterbirds.

ABOVE:
The Chesapeake Bay is an estuary
formed on the floodplain of the
Susquehanna River by the retreating
Ice Age.

As the time draws near when short days, chilling temperatures, frost, and ice will lay claim to northern wetlands, an inner restlessness quickens in many wading birds. In ponds and freshwater marshes, fish, once so accessible to spearlike bills, will soon swim dauntlessly beneath an impervious veneer of ice. The hum and buzz of insects will have long since ceased. The antics of fiddler crabs on saltwater mudflats will remain only a memory. Frogs, salamanders, snakes, and small mammals will lie huddled beneath logs, buried in mud banks, or coiled in hollow tree stumps, each deep in winter sleep.

With the impending decline in food supply and onslaught of inclement weather, wading birds migrate to more agreeable climes which, for northern populations, lie in a southern direction. For many species, such as the Great Blue Heron, only members of the northern populations are migratory; the southern populations are typically sedentary. Accordingly, Reddish Egrets, Roseate Spoonbills, and Wood Storks, which occur only in southern latitudes, have limited migration and are more or less year-round residents.

Since antiquity, poets, scholars, and children alike have beheld and questioned the seasonal comings and goings of birds. In the autumn, at least, it is easy to surmise that birds depart to regions where

Found from southern Canada through the United States, the white-tailed deer often frequents wetlands, especially swamps, where it grazes on aquatic vegetation.

Fossil evidence indicates that Sandhill Cranes, or close relatives, have been migrating through the Platte River valley of western Nebraska for at least 9 million years.

food remains available. The interesting question, however, is: Why do birds brave the rigors of long-distance travel to return north in the spring? Migration is risky business and energetically costly—about half of the autumn migrants will not live to return the following spring.

Again, food supply may be the answer. The cornucopia of prey—fish, aquatic invertebrates, insects, and other animals—that swim, fly, or crawl during the spring and summer in northern latitudes presumably draws birds like a magnet. In addition, the longer periods of daylight in the north permit more time to hunt for food, and predators may be relatively scarce. Thus, despite the energetic costs and dangers associated with intercontinental commutation, the rewards weigh heavily enough to have supported the evolution and maintenance of long-distance migration.

The first attempts to band North American birds to learn of their migratory wanderings were in 1902, and Black-crowned Night-Herons were the subjects. In that year, and in 1903 and 1910, Black-crowns from a Washington, D.C., heronry were banded with numbered rings. Subsequent recoveries yielded the first data on avian migratory movements of a North American species, and to date, great numbers of individuals of many avian species have been banded.

Members of the heron family are characteristically highly migratory. Even the Cattle Egret, a relative newcomer to the North American avifauna, migrates south from northern latitudes in the autumn. Both North American bitterns are impressive migrants. In fact, the first specimen of an American Bittern was discovered in England, an apparently misguided individual blown off course in a storm. Similarly, Green-backed Herons have turned up as vagrants on British shores at least twice.

Herons, as do most birds, follow major geographic migratory routes called flyways. Populations of east coast Great Blues, for instance, travel the Atlantic Flyway, while midwestern birds traverse the Mississippi Flyway. Obviously, it is crucial for survival that suitable wetlands occur throughout the migratory pathway.

Even before a heron's internal clock signals it to migrate in the autumn, extensive postbreeding dispersals may occur. These nomadic wanderings are especially typical of recently fledged birds and often result in significant journeys north of the natal area. Perhaps the youthful itinerants are seeking feeding areas where competition from adults is reduced. In situations where adults also disperse northward, perhaps they are seeking resource-rich areas that were unavailable dur-

In northern latitudes, the Yellow-crowned Night-Heron, like most species of long-legged wading birds, is highly migratory.

OVERLEAF PAGES:
At sunset, after a day of foraging, Sandhill Cranes return to roosting sites along the Platte River. In all, about five hundred thousand migrating cranes may populate the Platte valley in spring and autumn.

ing the early spring when breeding commenced farther south where the vernal thaw had already begun. Or maybe areas to the north have food resources but no nesting accommodations, and once the chores of nesting are complete, those resources can be exploited.

Regardless of the reasons for postnesting dispersal, it is a phenomenon often marked by dramatic movements. Little Blue Herons, Great Egrets, and Least Bitterns are occasionally sighted in Newfoundland. A Cattle Egret from California turned up in Alaska, and a southern Florida "Great White Heron" appeared in Pennsylvania. Black-crowned and Yellow-crowned Night-Herons also have extensive post-breeding wanderings. Not all herons, however, exhibit such marked movements: Reddish Egrets and Tricolored Herons, for example, show limited dispersals.

Other waders besides herons also exhibit wanderlust. The Glossy Ibis disperses extensively after the breeding season, and such travels may be responsible for the expanding range of this species. In fact, it is speculated that the Glossy Ibis, which R. S. Palmer describes as a chronic wanderer, may have spread from the Old World to the United States in the mid to late 1800s. This bronze-plumed traveler continues to extend its range both to the north and south: The first documented breeding attempt in Canada was made in New Brunswick in June 1986; in July 1988, breeding presumably occurred in southern Mexico.

White-faced and White Ibises also have significant postbreeding dispersals. However, whereas the former is highly migratory, the latter is mostly resident throughout its range. White-faced Ibises banded in Utah were documented wintering in the central highlands and coastal regions of Mexico. This migratory pattern, however, may have a cost in

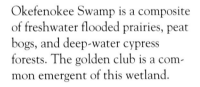

Okefenokee Swamp is a composite of freshwater flooded prairies, peat bogs, and deep-water cypress forests. The golden club is a common emergent of this wetland.

that those birds that winter in the interior agricultural region of Mexico show high levels of organochlorines and associated eggshell thinning.

Marked juvenile Roseate Spoonbills dispersed about four hundred kilometers from their south Florida natal area and returned during the fall. Spoonbills and Wood Storks are mainly year-round residents with little migratory movement. Wood Storks, however, disperse widely after nesting and may also travel afar after a failed nesting attempt due to drought or chilled temperatures. Limpkins are nonmigratory in their south Florida range.

The most notable migrants among North American long-legged wading birds are undoubtedly the cranes. Except for their Gulf coast populations, Sandhill Cranes perform spectacular long-distance migrations, mainly by day, and at times may fly so high that they are invisible from the ground. Studies have found that Sandhills can fly over five hundred and seventy kilometers nonstop in just under ten hours. In the spring and fall separate migrating flocks of fewer than four dozen birds congregate in the Platte River valley, often totaling more than five hundred thousand birds.

With their necks outstretched and their legs trailing behind, Whooping Cranes make an annual flight from their nesting grounds in Wood Buffalo National Park in Canada to their wintering habitat in Aransas National Wildlife Refuge in coastal Texas. The journey, with rest stops, takes about three weeks. Like harbingers of the wilderness, migrating cranes dominate the sky both visually and vocally as they link together distant reaches of the North American landscape. Sadly, the migration of Whooping Cranes, one of nature's most impressive displays, has almost disappeared from the face of the earth, for the wilderness, so stridently proclaimed and needed by the cranes, is vanishing.

4. Waders and Wetlands:

Past, Present, and Future

The history of wading birds in North America has not been without tribulations. During the late nineteenth and early twentieth centuries, life was especially tenuous for Snowy and Great Egrets. At that time the millinery trade was enjoying an unprecedented development, and plume-hunters were seeking their fortune by supplying the industry with feathers to adorn women's hats. Because of their long, delicate, immaculate white nuptial plumes, egrets were the favored target. The economic incentive was substantial, for in 1903 an ounce of aigrettes was valued at thirty-two dollars, or about twice the price of gold!

The industry demanded plumes from living birds since molted feathers were often soiled or damaged. Typically, hunters would begin shooting in the breeding season just after the eggs had hatched. Once the chicks were present, the adults would bond with the nestlings and were reluctant to abandon them despite the shooting. Thus, as a result of the whims of fashion and economic greed, entire egret colonies were wiped out.

By the turn of the century the number of Great Egrets was at an all-time low, and Snowys were on the verge of extinction in North America. Roseate Spoonbills, too, were nearly exterminated. The devastation inspired rallying cries from concerned citizens, which coalesced into one voice to form the National Association of Audubon Societies in 1905. With pressure from the association—which adopted the Great Egret as its symbol—and other groups, the New York legislature banned the sale of wild bird plumage in 1910, which put the plume-hunters out of business.

To date, the Snowy Egret has recovered from the devastation it experienced earlier in the century. In fact, it has extended its range beyond its previously occurring boundaries. The Great Egret, too, rebounded, but only until the mid-1930s. Then, although the menace of plume hunting was gone, an ever-increasing threat took precedence and continues to this day: the loss of wetland habitat.

Historically, the track record for conservation of wetlands has been poor at best. A recent report to Congress on the fate of wetlands from colonial times to the 1980s maintains that "the lower 48 states lost an estimated 53 percent of their original wetlands," which translates into a loss of "over 60 acres of wetlands for every hour between the 1780s and the 1980s." California holds the dubious distinction of being the state that has lost the highest percentage of original wetlands (91 percent), while Florida has lost the greatest total acreage (9.3 million acres). Alaska, in contrast, has lost less than 1 percent of its estimated 170 million acres of wetlands and is the state with by far the greatest expanse of these ecosystems.

What is the reason for this staggering loss of wetlands? For one thing, attitude. "Since the time of Colonial America," the report to Congress contends, "wetlands have been regarded as a hindrance to productive land use. Swamplands, bogs, sloughs, and other wetland areas were considered wastelands to be drained, filled, or manipulated." Moreover, the conversion of wetlands to agriculture, in the midwestern farm-belt states alone, has claimed 36 million acres, over 30 percent of the total lost since colonial times.

The elimination of wetlands did not go unnoticed by the federal government and was in fact encouraged. The first wetland policy of the United States was incorporated in the 1849 Swamp Land Act, which granted Louisiana authority to "reclaim" wetlands. In the following year twelve other states were included. Thus, with the federal government's blessing, the destruction of wetlands continued apace. States, too, acted independently to eradicate wetlands. Illinois, for example, passed the 1879 Illinois Drainage Levee Act and the Farm Drainage Act, which permitted the counties to drain almost all of the state's original wetlands.

Besides the relentless conversion to agricultural lands, particularly in the Midwest, wetlands have succumbed to a number of other threats, not least of which is urban development. Because greatest population densities occur in coastal areas, salt marshes and estuaries have been especially impacted by drainage and filling to build our cities and suburbs. Since 1850 about 95 percent of the tidal marsh area of the San Francisco Bay estuary has been lost. Other threats to wetlands have included pollution; pesticides; highway construction; canal building and dredging; peat, phosphate, and coal mining; oil drilling and shipping; pumping out of ground water; and recreational pressures.

Even though a wetland may appear intact, it may be seriously damaged. In parts of the Everglades, for example, agricultural runoff rich in nutrients from artificial fertilizers is altering water chemistry. Consequently, monocultural stands of cattails are invading and displacing naturally occurring sawgrass communities. By some estimates, almost five acres of sawgrass are lost daily. During the past two hundred years, the nature of wetland destruction in the United States has been such that the report to Congress concludes that "wetland acreage has diminished to the point where environmental and even socio-economic benefits . . . are now seriously threatened."

An obvious corollary of wetland destruction is the decline of wading birds. This linkage is clearly apparent in the case of the southern Florida ecosystem. In 1947 the Everglades, one of the most bountiful wetlands on the planet, was taken into the fold of the national park system. Ironically, since that time the Everglades has deteriorated significantly. As mentioned earlier, the integrity of this ecosystem depends on the sheet flow of fresh water from Lake Okeechobee, which lies to the north of the park. Unfortunately, much of the life-sustaining waters were, and continue to be, diverted via canals to the ocean to drain land for development and are impounded and pumped out for irrigation and urban water supplies. In addition, as mentioned above, runoff from cultivated lands introduced pollutants to the ecosystem. Consequently, many wetland acres in the Everglades have vanished forever and with them their wading birds. It is estimated that of the original population of nesting waders in southern Florida during the first half of this century, only 10 percent remains.

Perhaps the most impacted wading bird in the Everglades is the Wood Stork. In six decades its numbers have plummeted from an initial population of about several thousand breeding couples to a precarious two hundred or so pairs. Not only have many of its original habitats been diminished, its breeding attempts have been thwarted by untimely releases of water into the Everglades from managed impoundments to the north of the park. To secure enough food for its young, the Wood Stork depends on fish concentrated in drying ponds. When water is released from impoundments into the Everglades during the dry season, the bird's feeding habitat becomes inundated and the fish disperse. The decline in Wood Storks has been so dramatic that this imposing bird is now officially listed as an endangered species.

Habitat destruction has also led to the near demise of another of North America's endangered birds: the Whooping Crane. Although presumably never abundant—there are estimates of approximately two thousand birds existing prior to human impact—Whoopers nested throughout the wet prairies from the central United States through Canada. In the late 1800s settlers drained freshwater wetlands in Illinois, Iowa, Minnesota, and North Dakota in favor of wheat fields and cattle pastures. And, as if that were not enough, a crucial wintering range on the Louisiana prairies was also eliminated. In fewer years than it takes a Whooper to reach sexual maturity, millions of acres of Louisiana grasslands were converted to rice fields in the 1880s.

Besides the threat of habitat loss, Whooping Cranes faced other persecutions. Hunting and egg collecting each took its toll; in 1890 a Whooper skin fetched upwards of ten dollars and eggs were valued at two dollars each. Hunting just for the sake of the kill was another peril impacting Whoopers. Ultimately, during the final three decades of the nineteenth century, the Whooping Crane population crashed to roughly 10 percent of its original abundance, reaching a low of fewer than two hundred birds—a tragedy for one of North America's most statuesque birds and a pathetic testament to human negligence.

The crane population decline did not stop at the turn of the century, however. By the 1940s wild Whoopers numbered only twenty-one, a blink away from extinction. Fortunately, through concerted efforts of a number of dedicated individuals and conservation-minded groups, the Whooping Crane population has rebounded to just over two hundred at the time of this writing.

The decline of the Whooping Crane served as a conspicuous indicator of the state of our wetlands and the consequences of wetland loss. When wetlands go, the birds that depend on them go. Furthermore, perhaps in an initially less noticeable manner, the many ecological functions that wetlands provide also vanish. For example, many wetlands serve as regional "sponges," soaking up precipitation, intercepting storm runoff, and then slowly discharging these waters into the ground and into streams and coastal waters. Consequently, the risks of flooding are significantly mitigated. In addition, coastal wetlands, such as salt marshes and mangrove swamps, provide buffers against surging, pounding waves of storms, thus protecting shorelines from erosion.

Wetlands filter out pollutants from wastewater discharged into these ecosystems. Algae and bacteria, for instance, break down potentially noxious organic compounds into their innocuous constituents, while some emergent marsh plants remove heavy metals and other toxic substances from the water. The excess nutrient load of agricultural runoff can to some degree be absorbed by wetland vegetation. In addition, wetlands participate in the global cycling of elements, such as nitrogen and oxygen, that are crucial to the functioning of the biosphere.

The fact that natural wetlands exhibit water-purifying properties has led to the design and operation of "artificial" wetlands to cleanse sewage from municipalities. The use of man-made wetlands to treat sewage has met with encouraging success, most notably in facilities established in New England.

Besides providing important life-support functions, wetlands produce tangible resources. Timber harvesting, for example, sustains the economies of many communities in bottomland hardwood and cypress swamps of the Southeast. The prairie-pothole region of the Midwest supports the largest concentrations of waterfowl in North America. On the Pacific, Gulf, and Atlantic coasts, many commercial and sport fisheries rely on the fact that numerous fish species spend at least a part of their lives in wetlands. Other commercially valuable wildlife that are ecologically linked to wetlands include clams, mussels, blue crabs, crayfish, shrimp, alligators, and fur-bearers, such as muskrats. Clearly, wetlands have much to offer people, but these biological treasures must be conserved and managed wisely.

At no other time in history has the life-support system of our planet hung in such a precarious balance. Ecosystems ranging from tropical rain forests to coral reefs to old-growth forests to alpine tundra are facing monumental challenges that, taken collectively, threaten to unravel the tapestry of life on earth. As part of the fabric of that tapestry, the integrity of wetlands is crucial to the maintenance of the biosphere. And the fate of wetlands rests in our hands. What can be done?

First of all, it's important to note that much has been started. In 1903 President Theodore Roosevelt established the first U.S. National Wildlife Refuge on Florida's Pelican Island. Subsequently, the number of refuges multiplied so that in 1929, when Congress passed the Migratory Bird Conservation Act, a national wildlife refuge system was established. This network of protected areas, which is under the guardianship of the U.S. Fish and Wildlife Service, today has over four hundred thirty refuges encompassing more than 88 million acres. Although developed mainly for the purpose of waterfowl conservation, the national refuge system benefits many species of wading birds. Paralleling the history of U.S. refuges, Canada established its first bird refuge in 1887; about one hundred years later the Canadian Wildlife Service has about fifty national wildlife areas and twice that many migratory bird sanctuaries.

Besides the reserves managed by public agencies, numerous private organizations have purchased wetlands for protection. The National Audubon Society, for example, maintains an extensive network of wildlife sanctuaries, many of which include wetlands. The Nature Conservancy, by purchasing critical areas, has been important in the preservation of wetlands. In addition, conservation-minded private land owners and community nature reserves are safeguarding wetlands throughout the continent.

Wetlands have also received protection through federal government policies and laws. The 1970s saw major steps taken to conserve wetlands through the Coastal Zone Management Act (1972), Section 404 of the Federal Water Pollution Control Act (Amendments of 1972 and 1977; the latter also known as the Clean Water Act), and Executive Order 11990 issued by President Jimmy Carter, which mandated the stewardship of wetlands and riparian systems. States, too, passed legislation to protect wetlands, especially coastal areas. Unfortunately, inland wetlands typically are not given full consideration and presently remain more vulnerable than their coastal counterparts.

As a concerned citizen, there are numerous ways in which you can contribute to wetland conservation. Be informed about wetland issues and support legislation that defends these ecosystems. Write to local, state, and federal representatives urging them to consider protective measures. Exercise your influence at the November ballot box. Pledge support to conservation organizations and get involved in community projects, such as those sponsored by local chapters of the National Audubon Society. Help establish and maintain local nature preserves, and support community nature centers. Encourage schools to adopt programs in environmental education, and take your children to visit a marsh, pond, or swamp. And you can purchase duck stamps whose proceeds go directly into the acquisition and maintenance of federal refuges.

However, perhaps the most important commitment you can

The fate of the wetlands, and the abundance of life that dwells within them, rests in our hands. In just over two hundred years, since the time of European settlement, over half the wetlands of the continental United States have been lost. The choices and decisions we make in our everyday lives have direct impacts on the natural world. As we approach the twenty-first century, what choices will we make and how will they affect our wetlands?

make toward wetland conservation is to get to know one. Take the time to get acquainted with a wetland near home, school, or work place. Observe it through the seasons. Scoop up a handful of mud and squeeze it through your fingers. Identify its plants and animals, both large and small. Become familiar with the behaviors of its wading birds. Watch the life dramas that unfold among the various inhabitants. Cultivate a feeling for, and understanding of, the place. Your life will be enriched and at the same time a wetland and its wildlife will gain an advocate, a voice to speak for these ecosystems and the wading birds that grace them.

APPENDIX: Classification of Wading Birds

ORDER: CICONIIFORMES

Family: Ardeidae
American Bittern *Botaurus lentiginosus*
Least Bittern *Ixobrychus exilis*
Black-crowned Night-Heron *Nycticorax nycticorax*
Yellow-crowned Night-Heron *Nycticorax violaceus*
Green-backed Heron *Butorides striatus*
Tricolored Heron *Egretta tricolor*
Little Blue Heron *Egretta caerulea*
Reddish Egret *Egretta rufescens*
Snowy Egret *Egretta thula*

Cattle Egret *Bubulcus ibis*
Great Egret *Casmerodius alus*
Great Blue Heron *Ardea herodias*

Family: Ciconiidae
Wood Stork *Mycteria americana*

Family: Threskiornithidae
Glossy Ibis *Plegadis falcinellus*
White-faced Ibis *Plegadis chihi*
White Ibis *Eudocimus albus*
Roseate Spoonbill *Ajaia ajaja*

ORDER: GRUIFORMES

Family: Gruidae
Sandhill Crane *Grus canadensis*
Whooping Crane *Grus americana*

Family: Aramidae
Limpkin *Aramus guarauna*

BIBLIOGRAPHY

Allen, R. P. 1942. *The Roseate Spoonbill, Research Report of the National Audubon Society.* New York: Dover Publications.

———. 1952. *The Whooping Crane, Research Report of the National Audubon Society, No. 3.* New York: National Audubon Society.

Bent, A. C. 1963. *Life Histories of North American Marsh Birds.* New York: Dover Publications.

Bertness, M.D. 1992. "The ecology of a New England salt marsh." American Scientist 80: 260-68.

Dahl, T. E. 1990. *Wetlands Losses in the United States, 1780's to 1980's.* Washington, D.C.: U.S. Department of the Interior, Fish and Wildlife Service.

Day, J. W., Jr., C. A. S. Hall, W. M. Kemp, and A. Yanez-Arancibia. 1989. *Estuarine Ecology.* New York: John Wiley and Sons.

Doughty, R. W. 1989. *Return of the Whooping Crane.* Austin: University of Texas Press.

Eckert, A. W., and K. E. Karalus. 1987. *The Wading Birds of North America.* New York: Weathervane Books.

Ehrlich, P. R., D. S. Dobkin, and D. Wheye. 1988. *The Birder's Handbook: A Field Guide to the Natural History of North American Birds.* New York: Simon and Schuster.

Finlayson, M., and M. Moser, eds. 1991. *Wetlands.* New York: Facts on File, Inc.

Hancock, J. 1984. *The Birds of the Wetlands.* New York: Facts on File, Inc.

Hancock, J., and H. Elliott. 1978. *The Herons of the World.* New York: Harper and Row.

Hancock, J., and J. Kushlan. 1984. *The Herons Handbook.* New York: Harper and Row.

Johnsgard, P. A. 1983. *Cranes of the World.* Bloomington: Indiana University Press.

———. 1991. *Crane Music.* Washington, D.C.: Smithsonian Institution Press.

McNulty, F. 1966. *The Whooping Crane: The Bird That Defies Extinction.* New York: E. P. Dutton and Co.

Meyerriecks, A. J. 1960. *Comparative Breeding Behavior of Four Species of North American Herons.* Publ. Nuttal Ornithol. Club, no. 2.

———. 1962. "Diversity typifies heron feeding." *Natural History* 71(6):48-59.

Mitsch, W. J., and J. G. Gosselink. 1986. *Wetlands.* New York: Van Nostrand Reinhold.

Niering, W. A. 1985. *The Audubon Society Nature Guides. Wetlands.* New York: Alfred A. Knopf.

Palmer, R. S., ed. 1962. *Handbook of North American Birds,* Vol. 1. New Haven: Yale University Press.

Parnell, J. F., et al. 1988. "Colonial waterbird management in North America." *Colonial Waterbirds* 11:129-69.

Snyder, N. F. R., and H. A. Snyder. 1969. "A comparative study of mollusc predation by Limpkins, Everglade Kites, and Boat-tailed Grackles." *Living Bird* 8:177–223.

Soothill, E., and R. Soothill. 1982. *Wading Birds of the World*. Dorset, England: Blanford Press.

Sprunt, A., IV, J. C. Ogden, and S. Winckler, eds. 1978. *Wading Birds, Research Report of the*

National Audubon Society, No. 7. New York: National Audubon Society.

Teal, J., and M. Teal. 1969. *Life and Death of the Salt Marsh*. New York: Ballantine Books.

Terres, J. K. 1980. *The Audubon Society Encyclopedia of North American Birds*. New York: Alfred A. Knopf.

Voisin, C. 1991. *The Herons of Europe*. San Diego: Academic Press.

INDEX

Page numbers in *italics* refer to illustrations.